A NEW BEGINNING
Tertullian, Cyril, Augustine
on Baptism

WELLSPRINGS OF FAITH is a selection from the writings by Christians from the earliest times. The choice of texts introduces the reader to a range of the most notable and beautiful literature of the Christian tradition, a literature which can help Christians to deepen their faith and life of prayer.

This series Wellsprings of Faith (formerly Witnesses for Christ) is a project sponsored by A.I.M (Aide Inter-Monastères), an international organisation to serve the needs of young monastic communities in Africa and Asia. By providing patristic and monastic literature in an easily readable form, it hopes also to be of use to people throughout the English-speaking world.

Acknowledgments and thanks are due to a team of volunteer translators and others who have given their services.

WELLSPRINGS OF FAITH

vol xi

A NEW BEGINNING

Tertullian, Cyril, and Augustine
on Baptism

First published in 1998

Gracewing in conjunction with The Secretariat of
Fowler Wright Books Aide Inter - Monastères
2 Southern Avenue Leominster 7 Rue d'Issy
Herefordshire 92170 Vanves
HR6 OQF France

put into English by
Sr Mary Dominique OC Slough   Sr Mary Bernard OSB Fernham
D. Mary Groves OSB
revised from the Greek by Anthony Meredith SJ

All rights reserved. No part of this publication may be reproduced, stored in a retrieval system, or transmitted in any form, or by any means, electronic, mechanical, photocopying, recording or otherwise, without the written permission of the publisher.

© Aide Inter-Monastères 1997

The right of the editors and translators to be identified as the
authors of this work has been asserted in accordance with the Copyright,
Designs and Patents Act 1988

ISBN   0 85244 430 3

Typesetting by Kylemore Abbey
Connemara
County Galway

Printed by
Redwood Books, Trowbridge, Wiltshire BA14 8RN

Introduction vi

TERTULLIAN 1
On Baptism

Patrologia Latina 1107 - 1224

CYRIL OF JERUSALEM 36
Instruction after Baptism

Sources Chrétiennes no 126
St Cyril of Jerusalem : Lectures on the Christian Sacraments.
                                       St Vladimir Press

AUGUSTINE OF HIPPO 75
Easter Sermons

Sermones : 211 ; 212 ; 59 ; 227 ; 232
Patrologia Latina 38 : 1034 ; 1058 ; 400 ; 1099 ; 1107
Sermo Guelferbytanus 3
Sources Chrétiennes no 116

Introduction

In the early Christian centuries, new adult Christians were normally baptised during the Paschal Vigil on the night of Holy Saturday. They would be baptised and confirmed and receive Holy Communion for the first time, all in the same ceremony.

They would prepare for this great night by receiving instruction in the Faith. They were called Catechumens, from a greek word which means 'somebody who is receiving instruction.' Each Sunday during Lent, they would attend the Liturgy of the Word, the first part of the Eucharist. The Bishop would speak to them and teach them the Lord's Prayer (the 'Our Father') and the Creed. In the week after Easter they would come to the Church each day, wearing the white garments they had been given at their baptism, and they would be instructed about the meaning of the ceremonies of the Vigil during which they had been baptised. This instruction was called 'Mystagogy', which means 'introduction to the mysteries'.

The first three of the sermons of Augustine given in this book were preached by him during Lent, to instruct Catechumens. The third was preached on Good Friday, the fourth on Easter Day, and the fifth in the week after Easter. The sermons of Cyril of Jerusalem were all preached after Easter, to explain the Easter ceremonies.

Tertullian, or Quintus Septimius Florens Tertullianus, to give him his full name, was born to a non-christian family at Carthage in the Roman province of Africa around the year 160. He was well educated, and practised as a lawyer in Rome. Around 195 he returned to Africa, and became involved in the controversies of the African Church.

In his day, some people believed that the Hebrew Scriptures, which we know as the Old Testament, had nothing to do with Christianity. Tertullian wrote one of his longest books against them. In the book printed here he argues that baptism did not simply begin with Christianity, but was foreshadowed in the Old Testament.

Christians had suffered severe persecution in Africa, and many had fallen away from the Faith. The Church was divided : should the lapsed be admitted to the Church again after repentance, or should they be excluded permanently ? Parties who disagreed about this often refused to accept each other's baptisms as valid. The latter part of Tertullian's book *On Baptism,* printed here, is concerned with that question. It show Tertullian's clear, legal mind and his interest in controversy.

About the year 207 Tertullian left the Catholic Church and joined the sect of the Montanists, who emphasised the role of the Holy Spirit in the Church, and believed that those with outstanding spiritual gifts should exercise authority in the Church, not those who held ecclesiastical office. Tertullian died at Carthage some time after 220.

Cyril was ordained Bishop of Jerusalem in 348 at a time when the life of the Church was disturbed by the Arian controversy. He supported the doctrine of the Council of Nicea (325), but opponents of that Council twice forced him to leave his diocese. He was present in 381 at the Council of Constantinople, which gave to the Church the Nicene Creed in its revised form, very close to that now used in the Liturgy. He died in 387.

In Cyril's time, Jerusalem was a centre of rich liturgical life. A great basilica had been built over the site of Our Lord's Death and Burial, and pilgrims would travel to visit it and other sacred sites, and to take part in the liturgy of Holy Week, which commemorated Our Lord's Passion and Resurrection with visits to the places associated with them.

When the excitement of Holy Week was over, Cyril would gather those who had been baptised at Easter and explain the deeper meaning of the ceremonies in which they had taken part. The sermons printed in this book are the record of his explanations.

Augustine was born at Thagaste in North Africa in 354. He travelled to Rome to complete his education. He was a brilliant young man, dedicated to a life of pleasure, who began a literary career but was converted to Catholic Christianity under the influence of Saint Ambrose. He soon became a priest, and then returned to Africa as bishop of Hippo, where he remained until his death in 430. His writings fill many volumes. Some of them are commentaries on Scripture, and some are controversial works, for he entered into all the great theological controversies of his time. His best known book is the *Confessions*, in which he tells the story of his early life.

In the sermons printed in this book we can listen to Augustine as a pastoral bishop, explaining to those baptised at Easter the beliefs and way of life of Christians.

Bruce Harbert

TERTULLIAN

On Baptism

1. The water of Baptism gives life
2. Baptism amazes the human mind
   In praise of water
3. The Spirit of God was over the water
4. The evil spirit uses water
   The water in the pool of Bethsaida
5. God – Father, Son, Holy Spirit – and Baptism
6. The consecrated oil
7. The work of the Holy Spirit
8. Images of Baptism in the Bible

9. John's baptism
10. Christ's baptism
11. Did the apostles receive baptism?
12. Baptism is now law
13. Some declare: Paul did not baptise
14. Baptism among heretics
15. Baptism of blood
16. The one who baptises
17. Prudence necessary before giving baptism
18. When do you receive baptism?
19. How to prepare ourselves to receive Baptism
    Final advice

1 - THE WATER OF BAPTISM
GIVES LIFE

Praised be the Christian sacrament of water. *
This water washes away the sins we have committed
because at first we were blind.
It sets us free to live with God for ever.

This book will be useful to instruct the catechumens,
and also those Christians who were content to believe
without having received full teaching,
and so, because of their ignorance,
their faith remains weak and untried.
A short time ago,
a woman, poisonous as a viper, **
came to us here.

---

* This sacrament is Baptism. The Holy Spirit sanctifies the water and brings about the rebirth of the one baptised.
** Quintilla. The title of the book is : 'On Baptism, against Quintilla'. She spread a heresy in Carthage and taught that baptism by water is not necessary.

She belonged to a sect
and her teaching drew many away.
She fought especially against baptism.
Obviously that was her nature.
Like all serpents she preferred desert places
without water.

But we Christians are little fishes
like Jesus Christ who is our 'ictus'. *
We were born by water,
and we are saved only by remaining in this water.
That is why that horrible woman
who did not even have the right to teach,
found the best means of making these little fishes die
by removing them from the water.

2 - BAPTISM AMAZES THE HUMAN MIND

False teaching is very dangerous.
It attacks the roots of faith in order to destroy it,
or in order to stop us believing totally.
When God does things it appears simple
but he promises magnificent results.
The human spirit is quite unwilling to accept that.
Nevertheless, that is how baptism is performed.
It is all very simple, without exterior show.
No extraordinary setting is necessary
and no expense.
A person descends into the water and is sprinkled
while a few words are said.

---

* Ictus is a greek word meaning fish. In greek also, the five letters I.C.T.U.S. are the first five letters of the words: Jesus Christ Son of God, Saviour.

Tertullian

That person comes up out of the water
not much cleaner, if at all.
It seems all the more incredible, then,
that the result is eternal life.

Believe me,
it is quite different in the ceremonies, public or secret,
in honour of false gods,
for what raises their credibility and authority
is the show, the preparation and the expense.
What miserable incredulity is shown
by denying God's simplicity and power.
Is it not wonderful that a bath washes away death ?
Well, if it is too wonderful to believe,
that is all the more reason why you should believe.
For what should divine working be
if not more than wonderful.
So we ourselves wonder
but it is because we believe.
Others wonder and are incredulous
because they do not believe.
Besides, incredulous people wonder, but do not believe.
They wonder at simple things because they seem empty
and at great things because they are impossible,
and if you thinks this way
you only need to listen to the word of God
to find that it has answered you already.
'What the world finds foolish,
that God has chosen
to shame the wisdom of this world.' 1 Cor 1.27
And again:
'What is difficult for man
is easy for God.' Lk 18.17
For if God is both wise and powerful,

and even those who ignore him do not deny that,
it is with good reason that he chooses the opposite
of what is wise and powerful,
and uses what is foolish and impossible
as the material for his work.
Yes, strength always appears to greater effect
when something weak calls it into operation.

3 - WATER IN CREATION

While accepting the truth of these statements
I nevertheless go on to consider the question:
'How foolish and impossible it is to think
we can be formed anew by water.
How can this material substance, water,
be put to such an impossible use ?'
I suppose we should examine the fact that water is a liquid.
Indeed there has been plenty of evidence of this,
and from the very beginning.
For water is one of the things
which lay motionless under God's power
in a formless state,
before there was any suggestion of a created world.
The holy Bible says
that in the beginning God made the heavens and the earth.
When the earth was still not visible, still unformed,
and darkness was over the abyss,
the Spirit of God moved over the water. Gen 1.1,2

IN PRAISE OF WATER

We must first respect the age of the waters
because they are ancient,
and next the honour which God did them.
The Breath of God was upon them

Tertullian

and found them more pleasing than the other elements
at that time.
For the darkness was total,
shapeless and without stars to adorn it.
The abyss was gloomy,
the earth was unadorned,
the sky was not yet formed.
Only water was always a perfect substance,
joyful, simple, naturally pure, and giving life.
It was subject to God as a throne worthy of him.

Then, consider how God organised the world,
setting it in order by means of the waters.
To suspend the heavenly dome
he divided the waters in two,
and to suspend the dry land
he separated it from the waters.   Gen 1.6-8
Now that the world was in order, with its elements,
it was given its inhabitants.
First the command was given to the waters
to bring forth living creatures.
Water was the first to produce living things,
so it would be no cause for wonder
if the waters of baptism could give life. *
For water helped in the forming of man himself.
Earth was suitable matter for this
but not without being moistened and softened:
when the waters were separated out
and put in their proper place,
four days before man was formed,
they left some moisture which made mud.

---

*   This life given by the water of baptism is eternal life, lost by Adam's sin.
Gen 3. 22-24

If I go on to mention the many other things
which give this element its power or grace,
what is its role and ability, how useful it is to the world,
I fear you will think:
he praises water and forgets to speak to us of baptism..
However I have been able to show that without doubt
God used water in order to create all his works
and in the sacraments he also gives it the power
to enable us to be reborn.
Water governs life on earth: it also gives life for heaven.

4 - THE SPIRIT OF GOD WAS OVER THE WATER

All the points we have collected so far will be sufficient,
the most important being,
as we have already said,
that water is by its very condition a figure of baptism.
The Spirit of God who moved over the waters
will remain above those waters of baptism.
Assuredly one holy thing moved over another,
or rather, the water was changed to something holy
by the Spirit moving over it.
What is spiritual easily invades and penetrates
the whole substance of a material thing.
So the nature of water was made holy by the Holy Spirit
and received the power to sanctify, to make holy.

It is a simple action:
sin soils us, making us dirty,
and we are washed clean in water.
But sins do not appear on our flesh,
since no one bears on the skin the stain of idolatry

or fornication or fraud.
Yet sins dirty our soul which causes the sin,
for the soul commands and the body obeys,
However, both of them sin,
the soul because of what it commands,
the body because it obeys.
In the Gospel we read that there was a pool
and an angel came down on the water
and the water gave healing. Jn 5.4
In the same way, in the water of baptism
the soul is washed by means of the body
and the flesh is made spiritually clean.

5 - THE EVIL SPIRIT USES WATER

Those who do not believe in God
do not understand spiritual realities:
they imagine
that their false gods have the same power as the Holy Spirit
though the water they use is capable of nothing.
They learn the secrets of the false gods,
Thaïs perhaps or Mithras,
through water,
and they also give their gods a bath.
They sprinkle their villas, houses, temples,
and whole towns with water.
At the Games of Apollo and at Eleusis
they plunge into water.
They think that by doing this they receive new life
and all their dishonesty will go unpunished.
Among the ancients also,
anyone who had stained himself with murder
used to make himself pure by means of water.

Therefore if water is, by its very nature,
the proper thing for washing,
and for giving good omens and making the gods favourable,
as they tell themselves,
how much more true it is that water will do this
by the authority of God
who made all things.
If they think their religion gives water the power to heal,
faith in the living God is still more able to heal us.
Knowing this,
we see also that it is the Devil trying to be like God:
he imitates the things of God in baptising his own.
But is it the same thing?
Can the evil spirit, who is impure, make pure?
Can the destroyer set free?
He would be destroying his own work,
washing away the wrong-doing he himself inspires.

All these things are proofs against those who reject the faith
if they have no belief in the works of God
but prefer to believe those of God's enemy
who tries hard to imitate what God does.
Are there not other unclean spirits also who,
without any sacrament,
brood over waters,
trying to imitate the Spirit of God who brought things to life
at the beginning of the world.   Gen 1
There are shady springs and hidden streams
which know it well,
and it happens in bathing pools
and the channels and cisterns which are in houses, and wells,
which carry people off, they say,
by the power of harmful spirits.

They are drowned
or killed by plague or madness or swelling. *

THE WATER IN THE POOL OF BETHSAIDA

Why do I consider all these things?
It is so that you may believe this more firmly:
The holy angel of God is there
to sweeten water and enable it to save human beings,
just as the evil angel has unholy dealings
with the same element.
It may seem something new
that an angel should come down on the waters.
However we see an example of this
in the Gospel of John.   Jn 5.4
It was an angel who used to move the water
in the Pool of Bethsaida.
Those who were complaining of ill health
used to wait for the coming of the angel,
for whoever was the first to go down into the water
no longer had any complaint after washing.
Thus bodily healing is an image,
which tells of spiritual healing
according to the rule by which bodily things come first
and then the spiritual.
Thus God's grace makes progress in human beings
and does more by water and an angel
Formerly they were a remedy for bodily defects.
Now they are a medication for the soul,
now they give back eternal salvation.
Before, they gave freedom to one person once a year,

---

* In Tertullian's day it was, of course, not known how diseases breed in water.

now they save people every day.
Yes, baptism destroys death by washing away sins.
That is to say, when the guilt
of the accusation of sin is removed
the punishment is also removed.
Thus a human being is restored
to likeness to God.   Gen 1.26
Before, we were only in his image. *
We speak of an image as being like a form,
but the likeness we are speaking of is of God's eternity.
For we receive that Spirit of God
which he has given through his Breath of Life,
but which we had lost by sin.

6 - GOD — FATHER, SON, HOLY SPIRIT — AND BAPTISM

That is not to say
that we receive the Holy Spirit in the water,
but the water makes us pure
and so the work of the angel prepares us
to receive the Holy Spirit.
Here also, the image comes before the reality.
For as John the Baptist was the precursor
who came before the Lord to prepare his ways   Lk 1.76
so in the same way the angel,
who is witness to the baptism,
prepares the way for the Holy Spirit
who must come to wash away our sins.
This we receive through faith as we are sealed

---

* Tertullian is saying that we have been created in the image and likeness of God. The image of God we never lose. But sin makes us lose the likeness. Baptism gives us back likeness to God.

in the name of the Father, Son and Holy Spirit.   Mt 28.19
For if in the mouth of two or three witnesses
every word shall stand,   Mt 18.16
how much more are the three divine Names sufficient
to give assurance to our hope,
for through the blessing of Baptism
we have as witnesses of our faith
those who have promised that we shall be saved.
To the witness of the Three to our faith
and their promise of salvation must be added
the Church.
For where the Three are,
that is to say the Father, Son and Holy Spirit,
there is the Church which is the body of the Three.

7 - THE CONSECRATED OIL

After this, when we come out of the pool of baptism,
we are thoroughly anointed with the holy oil.
In the Old Testament, men who were to become priests
were anointed from a horn of oil.   Ex 30. 30
This is what Moses did for Aaron.
The name Christ came from this.
The meaning of 'chrismate' is to consecrate someone
by anointing that person with oil.
And so Christ is also a name of the Lord Jesus because,
by a spiritual anointing God the Father consecrated the Lord
by sending the Holy Spirit down upon him.   Mt 3.16,17
Also in the Acts of the Apostles we read:
'In that city, they were all gathered together against Jesus,
your holy servant whom you anointed.'   Acts 4.27

So, for us also, oil flows over our bodies,
but it is our souls which benefit from it.

Tertullian

It is the same for the baptismal water:
our body is plunged in it
but it is our soul which is freed from sin.

8 - THE WORK OF THE HOLY SPIRIT

Then the priest places his hands on us,
he blesses us and at the same time calls down the Holy Spirit.
Human skill can certainly bring a breath of air (spiritus)
into water and there is an instrument, the organ,
in which water and breath are brought together
in the body of the instrument
and a musician, by playing on it with his hands,
can call forth another breath of such clear sound.
So, cannot God, through holy hands laid on his organ, *
play the marvellous music of the Holy Spirit ?

To place hands on someone is also an ancient sacrament.
Jacob, in order to bless his little grandsons,
Ephraim and Manasseh the sons of Joseph,
placed his hands on their heads
and blessed them. Gen 48. 13,14
He crossed his hands, slanting one over the other,
and so his arms made the shape of Christ's cross
His hands were an announcement of the blessing
which would come through Christ.
Then that most holy Spirit, sent by the Father,
comes down on the cleansed and blessed bodies,
and he remains on the baptismal water
as though recognising his kingly throne of earlier times. **

---

* Tertullian is speaking of a musical instrument, a kind of organ, which was played through the use of water and air. God's organ is the person baptised by the priest. ** see chapter 4 page 10

Tertullian

He descended on the Lord
in the form of a dove,   Mt 3.16
so that the nature of the holy Spirit may be revealed
through this bird's simplicity and innocence.
The dove has no gall-bladder in its body
and so, no bitterness.
That is why it is said in the Gospel:
'Be as straightforward as doves.'   Mt 10.16
And even that statement of the Lord's
is connected with an earlier image.
For just as all the sins from former times
were washed away in the great Flood,
so after the Baptism, one could say, of the world,
that a dove sent out from the ark was the herald
announcing the end of the heavenly wrath,
and came back with a little olive branch.
Even among the pagans the olive branch
represented peace.
In the same way, but in a spiritual manner,
when our earth, that is to say our body,
comes up from the bath of baptism
washed from its sinful ways,
the Holy Spirit flies towards us like the dove
coming from heaven and bringing God's peace.
The Church is represented by Noah's ark.   1 Pet 3 20-21

But you are going to say:
Human beings have continued to commit sins,
so the comparison with the great flood is not very good.
Indeed, this is why the world will be destroyed by fire,
and so will those who after baptism
return to their sins.   2 Pet 3.7
And so too we must understand this as a warning to us

9 - IMAGES OF BAPTISM IN THE BIBLE

There are many images throughout the Old Testament
of the water of baptism.
The people crossed the water of the Red Sea   Ex 14.27-30
and escaped from the power of the egyptian king,
and the water extinguished the king and all his army.
What image could more clearly present
the sacrament of baptism ?
Indeed, the nations are delivered from the world of evil
through baptism.
They turn away from the evil spirit, their old master,
who is overthrown in the water.

Moses plunged a piece of wood into bitter water
and gave it back its proper sweetness.   Ex 15.24,25
That was the wood of Christ on the cross.
Christ of himself healed the poisoned and bitter water of nature
and made it into the water of baptism.
It is the water which flowed down from the rock
which accompanied the Hebrews in the desert.   Ex 17.6
For if Christ is our rock,   1 Cor 10.4
then without doubt we see
that the water of baptism is blessed in Christ.

How much grace water has for conferring baptism
in the sight of God and his Christ.
Christ is always accompanied by water
since Jesus himself
was baptised in the water of the Jordan.   Mt 3.13
It was the first element to give proof of his power.
When he was invited to the marriage at Cana
he changed water into wine.   Jn 2.7

When he was speaking to the crowd he invited the thirsty
to drink his everlasting water.   Jn 4.14
When he was teaching about love,
he praised a cup of water offered to another
as one among the works of charity.   Mt 10.42
When he was tired, he rested by a well.   Jn 4.6
He walked on the water,   Jn 6.19
he crossed freely over the water of the lake.   Mt 14.34
With water he washed the feet of his disciples.   Jn 13..5
The witness of water to baptise continues in his Passion:
when he was condemned to die on the cross
water was still there –
Pilate washed his hands with water.   Mt 27.24
And when the soldier pierced his side with a lance,
water gushed out.   Jn 19.34

10 – JOHN'S BAPTISM

So far, I have tried to tell in general of all the things
which support the sanctity of baptism.
Now I am going to answer to the best of my ability
certain additional questions
which are asked on the subject of baptism.
The Lord himself asked the Pharisees a question
about the baptism announced by John:
"Did the baptism of John come from heaven
or was it of human origin ?"   Mt 21.25
The Pharisees were not able to give a straightforward answer.
They did not understand because they did not believe.
But I, in spite of my small intelligence and little faith,
am able to give the answer:
John's baptism was from God, because he was sent by God,
though not with full power.

Tertullian

In the Gospel we read
that John was sent by God to baptise,   Jn 1.33
but as a man among men,
and for that reason he did not give the heavenly baptism
but prepared the people for the things of heaven.
That is, he called them to repent,
and that human beings can do.
And then the Masters of the Law and the Pharisees
refused to believe and change their way of life.
But if to repent is human,
necessarily the baptism of John was also human.
If it had been heavenly
it would have given the Holy Spirit and forgiveness of sins.
But only God can take away sin   Mk 2.7
and give the Holy Spirit.   1 Thess 4.8
And the Lord himself said
that unless he himself first ascended to the Father
the Holy Spirit would not descend.   Jn 16.7
What the Lord had not yet given
the servant could not give either.
And so afterwards, in the Acts of the Apostles, we find
that those who received John's baptism
had not received the Holy Spirit.
They had not even heard of him.   Acts 19.2
What therefore did not give heavenly things
was not from heaven.
When that which was heavenly in John,
the spirit of prophecy,
left him after the Spirit transferred completely to the Lord,
John, who had preached him
and had pointed him out as the one who was to come,
sent to know whether he was the one.   Mt 11.2-6
In this way the baptism of repentance
called for the forgiveness and sanctification

that were to come in Christ.
For the baptism of repentance for the forgiveness of sins
which John was preaching   Mk 1.4
was a declaration of the forgiveness to come.
If penitence comes first, forgiveness follows.
This is what is meant by 'preparing the way'.   Lk 1.76
The one who prepares is not the same
as the one who brings to perfection,
but he makes possible for the other to make perfect.
John himself admits that the heavenly things are not his
but belong to Christ
when he says, speaking about himself and Christ,
"The one who comes from the earth
speaks about earthly things;
the one who comes from above
is above all."   Jn 3.31
Again, he said:
"I baptise for repentance.
Soon another is going to come
and he will baptise you with the Spirit and fire.'   Mt 3.11
That is to say that true and stable faith
is baptised in water for salvation,
but pretended and weak faith is baptised in fire
for judgment.

11 – CHRIST'S BAPTISM

Then some say:
"The Lord came and he did not baptise."
Indeed we read:
'It was not Jesus himself who baptised
but his disciples.'   Jn 4.2
But it was not as though John proclaimed:
'Jesus himself will baptise with his own hands.'

Tertullian

That is certainly not what is to be understood
by his words. Mt 3.11-13
They must be understood simply,
according to the ordinary way of speaking,
as when one says for example:
'The emperor has drawn up a law',
or again: 'The officer beat him with rods'.
Does the emperor himself draw up the law ?
Does the officer give the beating ?
They are always said to do it
because they give the order for it to be done.
That is how it is to be understood.
'He will baptise you' stands for:
You will be baptised for him or in him.
No one should be surprised
that Christ did not himself baptise.
What is he to baptise for ?
For repentance ?
Why then did he have John as the Precursor ?
For forgiveness of sins,
when he can do this with a word ?
In his own name ?
But Jesus was, by humility,
concealing who he was. Jn 6.15
Baptise in the Holy Spirit ?
But the Spirit had not yet come down
from the Father. Jn 15.16
Baptise into the Church ?
But it had not yet been begun by the Apostles.
And so Christ's disciples did the baptising as his ministers,
the same baptism as John performed earlier.
No one should think any other baptism existed.
There was no other
except that which Christ would establish later. Mt 28.19

The apostles could not give it then of course
because Christ had not yet entered into his glory.
It was his Passion and Resurrection
which gave baptism its power.
Nothing can destroy our death
except the Lord's Passion;
nothing can restore us to life
except his Resurrection. Rom 6.3-10

12 – DID THE APOSTLES RECEIVE BAPTISM ?

We are instructed
that no one can be saved without baptism.
This is based chiefly on that saying of the Lord:
'No one not born of water will have life.' Jn 3.5
As a result some people express anxious doubts,
or rather, bold denials,
and ask how the Apostles obtained salvation,
according to this instruction.
'We do not find that any of them received baptism in the Lord
except Paul.'
Or rather, since Paul is the only apostle among them
who received baptism in Christ,
'Were the rest who lacked the water of Christ
in danger of judgment,
if the instruction is right ?'
Or : 'The instruction is cancelled
if people who have not been baptised can be saved.'
I have heard, the Lord knows, things of that kind.
Do not think that I would be so dishonest as to invent things
as I write, and cause doubts in others.

And now I will reply as well as I can
to those who say the Apostles were not baptised.
Suppose they had undergone the human baptism of John
and then wanted the Lord's baptism.
But the Lord himself has said
there is only one baptism. Eph 4.5
He said this when he said to Peter,
who did not want to be washed
and then wanted to be washed all over, Jn 13.10
"One who is washed does not need to be washed again."
He would not have said that
to someone who had not been baptised.
So this is the obvious proof against those
who want to forbid baptism
by saying that the Apostles did not receive
the baptism of John.
Can it seem believable
that the way of the Lord was not yet prepared,
by John's baptism,
in those who were chosen to open the way of the Lord
in the whole world ?
The Lord himself was baptised and yet he had no sin.
Then is it not necessary for sinners to be baptised ?

And were there not others who were not baptised ?
They were not companions of Christ
but enemies of the faith.
These were the Masters of the Law and the Pharisees.
So then, while the enemies of Christ
did not want to be baptised,
those who followed the Lord accepted baptism
and did not react as did his adversaries,
especially since the Lord whom they loved
praised John the Baptist by saying:

"There has been none greater among those born of women
than John the baptiser." Mt 11.11

Again, others say, plainly forcing the interpretation somewhat,
that the Apostles fulfilled the requirement of baptism
when the waves washed over them
in their little boat; Mt 8.24
and the same thing for Peter
when he walked on the water,
and got wet enough. Mt 14.28,29
In my opinion however
it is one thing to be sprinkled or covered
by the waves of the sea,
and another to be baptised during a ceremony.
On the other hand, the Apostles' boat
when it was tossed by the waves
did give a picture of the Church
tossed by persecution and temptation
on the agitated sea of the world,
while the Lord remains patient and asleep
until roused by the prayers of the saints in extreme danger.
He restrains the world
and restores peace to his own. Mt 8.24

Now, either the Apostles received baptism in some form,
or they lived all their lives without being baptised.
In that case,
the word of the Lord to Peter about being washed
does concern us. Jn 13.10
But to want to judge whether the Apostles were saved or not
is rather bold,
because they had the honour to be the first to be chosen
and afterwards to live in close companionship with Christ,
and that could be a short cut to baptism I think.

For they were following Christ,
and it was he who promised salvation
to all who believe in him.
He would say: "Your faith
has saved you,"   Mt 9.22; Lk 18.42; Mk 10.52
and "Your sins are forgiven,"   Mk 2.5
to any people who had faith,
though they had not received baptism.
If the Apostles did not have faith
I do not know who had.
At one word of the Lord,
one got up from his desk,   Mt 9.9
another left his father and their boat
and the trade by which he made his living.   Mt 4.21,22
One who did not wait to bury his father
carried out the Lord's highest command before he heard it:
'The one who loves his father or mother more than me
is not worthy of me.'   Mt 10.37

13 – BAPTISM IS NOW A LAW

Here now, some very bad people
want to raise doubts about this
and so they say baptism is not necessary
for those whose faith is sufficient,
for Abraham pleased God not by any sacrament of water
but by the sacrament of faith.   Gen 15.6
But in all things,
what comes last is the conclusion,
and what follows is more important than what went before.
Before the Passion and Resurrection of the Lord
no doubt salvation was by faith alone.
But where faith has extended to include
belief in his Birth, Passion and Resurrection,

the sacrament of faith is enriched
and the seal of baptism is added to it.
That seal of baptism is, so to say, clothing for a faith
which before was bare.
And now it cannot be without its proper law,
that is to say, the law of baptism.
For the Lord imposed the law of baptism,
and with the prescribed form,
when he said : Mt 28.19
'Go and teach the nations. Baptise them
in the name of the Father, the Son and the Holy Spirit.'
Alongside this law is set the explanation:
'No one shall enter the kingdom of heaven
without being born of water and the Holy Spirit.' Jn 3.5
This faith is firmly linked to the necessity of baptism.
Therefore, since then,
all those who believe
have been baptised,
and the Apostle Paul himself received baptism
when he believed. Acts 9.18
And that is what the Lord had ordered him to do
when he was blinded, saying: Acts 9.3-8
"Get up and go to Damascus.
There it will be shown to you
what you have to do", Acts 22.10
that is to say, receive baptism.
It was the only thing he lacked.
For the rest, he had earned enough,
and he believed Jesus of Nazareth to be the Lord,
the Son of God.

14 – SOME DECLARE PAUL DID NOT BAPTISE

But these people fall back on what Paul himself said:
"Christ did not send me to baptise." 1 Cor 1.17
as though this was a reason to do away with baptism.
For, why did he baptise Caius and Crispus
and the household of Stefanus ? 1 Cor 1.14,16
However, even if Christ did not send him to baptise
he had commanded the other Apostles to do so.
But Paul was writing to the Christians of Corinth
because divisions and arguments were rising among them.
One said: 'I am for Paul',
another: 'I am for Apollos'. 1 Cor 1.12; 3.4
Paul was a peacemaker
and he did not wish to appear to have responsibility
for all the church services.
He says he had not been sent to baptise
but to preach. 1 Cor 1.17
In my opinion,
one who has the right to announce the Gospel
has also the right to baptise.

15 – BAPTISM AMONG HERETICS

I do not know if any further point is raised
in the baptism controversy.
It will be well if I review
what I omitted above
in case I seemed to interrupt the sense
of what I was about to say:

For us there is only one baptism,

whether in the Lord's Gospel *
or in the Letters of the Apostle Paul.
For there is one Lord, one baptism
and one church in the heavens.   Eph 4.4-6

But what is to be the rule about heretics ?
Certainly it is worth considering,
for what they say contradicts us.
But the heretics do not follow our rules.
They have broken away from us
and are strangers to us.
I do not have to recognise in them
the commandment given to me
because their God is not our God,
nor do we have the one, that is the same, Christ.
Therefore we do not have the one baptism
and so they do not receive it,
and what they have is not to be recognised at all.
This I have dealt with more fully in Greek.
Therefore we bathe once in baptism
and our sins are washed away once
because we ought not to repeat them.
Yet the Jewish people of Israel wash daily   see Mk 7.1-4
because each day
they need to purify themselves again.   Jn 13.10
In case the same should be done by us also
it has been decided that this washing takes place once only.
This is a good water
which washes once and for all,
which is not a mockery for sinners,
which is not infected by any number of impurities,
so staining those it has washed.

---

* see chapter 12

16 – BAPTISM OF BLOOD

We are able to be baptised in another way,
and this also once only.
It is the baptism of blood. *
The Lord spoke of it when he said:
"I have a baptism
with which I am to be baptised."   Lk 12.50
And yet he had already been baptised.
As the Apostle John writes,
he had come by water and blood.   1 Jn 5.6
He received baptism by water, glory by the Blood, **
so that he could enable us to be called by water,
chosen by the Blood.   Rev 17.14
He gave these two baptisms
from the wound in his pierced side.   Jn 19.34
Those who believe in his Blood
may be washed in the water,
and those who have been washed in the water
may also drink the Blood.   Jn 6.53
Baptism of blood takes the place of water
when that has not been received,
and restores it when it has been lost.

17 – THE ONE WHO BAPTISES

To conclude this little book,
it remains to speak of the rules
for giving and receiving baptism.
The right to give baptism belongs to the chief priest
who is the bishop.

---

*   That is, martyrdom.
**   Christ's Blood, that is, his Passion and death on the cross.

Tertullian

After him, the priest and deacons,
but not without the approval of the bishop.
To respect the bishop is to respect the Church.
When that is maintained, peace is maintained.

In addition, lay people also have the right.
For what they have received as equals,
they may give as equals.
They are called to do it
unless bishops, priests or deacons are present.
The Lord's word should not be kept hidden from anyone.
And so baptism, equally regarded as coming from God,
can be performed by all.
Nevertheless the first who has power is the bishop.
And simple Christians, even more than the priests,
must respect that power
and not make themselves into bishops.
Rivalry is the mother of schism.
The most holy Apostle Paul wrote:
'All things are lawful
but not all things are expedient.' 1 Cor 10.23
That is to say,
let it be sufficient for you to make use of this power
whenever the place, the moment, or the state of a person
asks for it.
For heroism is shown by those giving aid
when the circumstances are urgent and dangerous,
whereas it will result in the loss of a human being
if a person avoids fulfilling what could be freely done.

However the boldness of that woman
who takes it upon herself to teach *

---

* Quintilla. see p5, p6

will certainly not bear her the right to baptise herself,
unless she produces some new animal like the earlier one;
for if anyone thinks that writing,
which is attributed to Paul, *
defends the example of Thecla
as giving permission to women to teach and baptise,
let them know that the priest in Asia (Minor)
who composed that account,
as though he could add to Paul's title to fame,
(he said he did it for love of Paul)
has been convicted
and removed from his office....

18 – BEFORE GIVING BAPTISM IT IS NECESSARY TO BE PRUDENT

However, those whose duty it is
know baptism is not to be given with hasty trustfulness.
'Give to all who ask you'   Lk 6.36
rightly belongs under the heading of giving alms.
But this, rather, is what we should look at :
'Do not give what is holy to dogs
and do not throw your pearls to the pigs' ;   Mt 7.6
and : 'Do not be hasty in the laying on of hands
in case you share in another's sin.'   1 Tim 5.22

---

* 'The Acts of Paul and Thecla'. This fictitious account of St Paul's apostolate and death includes an account of Thecla, supposedly a noble virgin of Iconium who was converted by Paul, preached the Gospel, was miraculously saved from martyrdom many times and finally baptised herself in the arena.

Tertullian

If Philip baptised the eunuch so quickly,   Acts 8.26-40
we recognise that a clear statement of his worthiness
had come from the Lord.
The Holy Spirit told Philip to take that road.
And the eunuch himself is not idle,
nor like someone asking for baptism all of a sudden.
He had gone to the Temple to pray
and was reading the Holy Scriptures attentively.
It was fitting that he should be found doing this.
Besides, God had sent the Apostle to him
and, again, the Spirit ordered him
to join the eunuch in his chariot.
The Scripture came at the right time
to increase his faith,
he received instruction, he was shown the Lord,
he made no delay in believing,
he did not have to wait for water and,
the baptism completed,
the Apostle was snatched away.
Paul too was baptised very speedily.
For his host Simon quickly recognised him to be
an appointed vessel of election. *

God gives signs in advance of a person's worthiness.
Those who ask for baptism can mislead
and be misled.
Therefore it is better to wait a while,
and take account of the circumstances and dispositions
and even the age of each person,

---

*   It was in fact a man called Judas with whom Paul stayed (Acts 9.11). St Peter stayed with Simon   (Acts 9.43).   It was Ananias who baptised Paul and recognised him to be a chosen instrument (Acts 9.15).

Tertullian

especially where children are concerned.
For what need is there
for the sponsors themselves to be endangered ? *
They themselves may die
and be unable to fulfil their promises,
or again, they may fail
in preventing evil tendencies in the children as they grow up.
It is true, the Lord said: "Let the little children come to me;
and do not stop them."   Mt 19.14
Yes, let them come, but when they are older.
Let them come when you are able to teach them,
when they will learn to know the One to whom they come.
Let them become Christians
when they are capable of knowing Christ.
Why should the age of innocence
be in a hurry for the remission of sin ?
We act more cautiously about the affairs of the world.
We do not entrust earthly goods to a child,
yet we entrust them with the goods of heaven.
Let them know how to ask for salvation
so that you will be seen to be giving to those that ask it....

19 – WHEN DO YOU RECEIVE BAPTISM ?

The great day to receive baptism is Easter Day
when the Lord's Passion is complete,
for it is in that Passion that we are baptised.
It is interesting that when the Lord
was about to enact the Last Passover
he sent his disciples to prepare saying :

---

*   In Tertullian's day, infant baptism was not as normal as it now :
we think of it as helping the child to resist sin as it grows older.
Some people still today agree with Tertullian's argument. In the
early Church, St Cyprian especially did not agree.

"You will meet a man carrying a jar of water."   Mk 14.13
So he points out the place for celebrating the Pasch
by the sign of water.

Another time which is also very suitable
is between Easter and Pentecost.
During that time
the risen Lord was often with his disciples.   Acts 2
They were looking forward to the coming of the Spirit
and the hope of the second coming of the Lord.
He was received into the heavens
and the angels told the disciples
that he will come again in the same way
as they saw him go into heaven.   Acts 1.11
And of course on Pentecost Sunday is a good time.
When the prophet Jeremiah declares:
"I shall gather them
from one end of the earth to the other"   Jer 31.8
on the day of festival,
it means the time between Easter and Pentecost
which is all one festival.

However, every day belongs to the Lord, and every hour.
Every time is a good time for baptism.
Even if a feast day gives the ceremony more importance,
it makes no difference to the grace received.

20 – HOW TO PREPARE OURSELVES TO RECEIVE BAPTISM

Those who want to receive baptism ought to turn to God
in prayer often, in fasting, in kneeling
and in watching in prayer to God through the night.
And this together with confession

of all the sins of their past life
so that they give expression to the baptism of John.
Scripture says:
'They were baptised, confessing their sins.' Mt 3.6
We should be grateful
that we do not make public confession
of our sins and misdeeds. *
At one and the same time we do penance
by mortification of our flesh and our spirit,
and prepare beforehand for a defence against temptation,
which will soon come.
'Watch and pray', the Gospel says,
'so that you do not enter into temptation.' Mt 26.41
I believe that the disciples were tempted
because they fell asleep,
and that was why they deserted the Lord
when he was arrested.
Even the one who remained with him
and tried to defend him with a sword,
nevertheless afterwards denied Jesus
three times. Mt 26.31
For it had been already said
that no one who has not been tempted
will enter the heavenly kingdom. see Jas 1.12
The Lord himself, immediately after his baptism,
was surrounded by temptations
during his forty days fast.
Some will say :
" So we too ought to fast after our baptism ? "

---

* Tertullian may have been thinking of actual public confession, as customary in some of the early Church congregations; or he may have been thinking of Prov 28.13 : by confessing now we shall not have to do so publicly at the Last Judgment.

Tertullian

And what is there to stop you, except that
you must be rejoicing and giving thanks
because we have been saved.
But the Lord, as I see it,
figuratively turned on himself the reproach against Israel.
For the people crossed the sea and wandered in the desert
during forty years,
and there God fed them,   Ex 16.5
yet the people thought more of their mouths and stomachs
than of God.   Num 21.5
And as the Lord,
by going alone into the desert after the water of baptism
and fasting forty days,
has shown that a man of God does not live on bread alone
but on the word of God,   Mt 4.4
and that the temptation to eat too much
is overcome by imposing abstinence on our stomach.

FINAL ADVICE TO THOSE WISHING TO RECEIVE BAPTISM

Therefore blessed are those for whom grace is waiting.
When you rise up from the most holy bath of your new birth,
for the first time you will go with your brethren
to lift your hands in prayer in the house of the Church,
your Mother.
Then ask the Father, ask the Lord,
for special gifts and graces to be distributed.
"Ask and you will receive", he said.   Mt 7.7
So, you have sought and you have found,
you have knocked and the door has been opened to you.

> Only, now when you are asking,
> do not forget to pray also for :
> > Tertullian, a sinner.

CYRIL OF JERUSALEM

Instruction after Baptism

Now you are a Christian   38
    (Catechesis 1)

Understand your baptism   45
    (Catechesis 2)

The signing with Holy Oil   51
    (Catechesis 3)

Reception of the Eucharist   58
    (Catechesis 4)

The Eucharistic Celebration   62
    (Catechesis 6)

1
NOW YOU ARE A CHRISTIAN
1 Peter 5. 8-14

In this first instruction, Cyril explains to the newly Baptised the ceremonies which took place before they were baptised. The catechumens were brought to the outer hall of the baptistery. There they made a solemn promise: they renounced the spirit of evil and all that belongs to him, then they promised to remain always faithful to Jesus Christ.

Cyril quotes from the Greek text of the Bible, often different from the Latin text. The Psalms are given here first with the number from the liturgical psalter, then with the number from the Hebrew Bible.

YOU ARE CHILDREN OF THE CHURCH

1 You have become true children of the Church.
  She has longed very much for your coming.
  And for a long time I have wanted to explain to you
  the mysteries which come from the Spirit of God. *
  But I know it is easier to believe what you see
  rather than what is only heard.
  That is why I have waited until this season.
  Now you are much better prepared from experience
  to follow me in all that I am going to say.
  Starting from that all-important night,
  I am going to lead you, as though by the hand,
  right into the meadow of our wonderful garden, **
  so full of light and perfume.

---

*   The sacraments of christian initiation: Baptism, Confirmation, Eucharist.
** Paradise, to be found in the mysteries themselves. The baptised Christian discovers the joy of that Paradise which God had prepared for our first parents. (Gen 2)

Cyril of Jerusalem

You are now capable of understanding
the depths of these mysteries
through Baptism which gives you new life ......
So you will understand the deep meaning
of the ceremonies carried out on the night of your baptism.

2 First you came into a hall just outside the baptistery.
There, turned toward the west, you listened. *
And a voice said : Stretch out your hand.
Then you renounced Satan as though he was present.

AS GOD FREED THE HEBREWS, SO HE FREED YOU

You ought to know this :
What you have done is already foretold
in the history of God's people.
Pharaoh, king of Egypt, indeed a cruel and wicked ruler,
made the Hebrews his slaves,
although they were a freeborn and noble people.
God sent Moses
to release them from their slavery to the Egyptians.
The Hebrews marked their doorposts with the blood of a lamb
and the destroying angel passed over the houses
marked with this sign.   Ex 12.21,22
And so God freed the Hebrews in a marvellous way.
When Pharaoh wanted to pursue those who had been freed,
he saw the sea open up in front of them,
again in a marvellous way.
However, he continued to follow after them,
but suddenly the Red Sea flowed back again
and the enemy were drowned.   Ex 14.22-30

---

* To the west, because Satan is darkness and directly opposed to Christ who is thought of as the rising sun. The early Christians made an act of renunciation of Satan as we still do at baptism and the Easter Vigil, and also lifted their hand in defiant opposition to him, and to swear it on oath.

Moses is a type of Christ

3 Now come with me from ancient history to the present,
from types and images to the reality.
There we have Moses sent by God into Egypt,
here we have Jesus Christ sent by his Father into the world.
There, Moses had to lead the slaves out of Egypt,
here Christ has to free us, weighed down by sin in this world.
Then, the blood of the lamb
prevented the destroying angel from acting,
now the precious blood of Christ,
the Lamb without blemish, 1 Pet 1.19
protects us against the evil spirits.
There, cruel Pharaoh pursued the Hebrews right into the sea,
here, the devil, who feels no shame and fears nothing,
who is the source of all evil,
pursued you right into the waters of salvation.

Satan is darkness

4 So then, you were told to stretch out your hand and say,
as though he was present : ' I renounce you, Satan.'
You turned towards the west. Why is that ?
I am going to explain this to you as it is important.
As you know,
the west is the region of darkness, where the sun sets.
And Satan is darkness :
he exercises his power in the darkness of night.
That is why you looked to the west.
It is a sign that you renounce the prince of darkness and evil.
And after this, what did you say, one after the other ?
You said : I renounce you, Satan, wicked and cruel taskmaster.
You were saying : I am no longer afraid of you.
Christ has destroyed your power
by taking flesh and blood like mine.

He has destroyed death by dying himself.   Heb 2.14,15
And as for me, I am freed from your slavery for ever.
I renounce you, scheming and lying serpent.   Gen 3.1
I renounce you deceitful spirit.
Pretending to be friendly, you worked all your evil schemes
and you persuaded our first parents to disobey.
I renounce you, Satan,
plotter of evil schemes and carrying them out through us.

SATAN URGES YOU ON TO DO WHAT IS WICKED

5 Then, you were taught to say this :
'And I renounce all your works.'
The works of Satan : that means all kinds of sin.
You must renounce them : it is absolutely necessary.
You are like someone who has escaped from a cruel master
and throws away the arms he carried in his service.
Oh yes, the works of the evil spirit are involved in all sin.
Furthermore, remember this well :
Everything you said in that solemn moment
is written in God's books.   Rev 20.12
And so if you do something against your promises
you will be considered a sinner.   Gal 2.18
That is why I tell you to renounce the works of Satan,
that is to say all the deeds and thoughts
which go against your promise.

6 Then you said : 'I reject all the unworthy pastimes
which the spirit of evil makes us think are so attractive.'
For example, it could be a passion for shows, *
horse-racing, hunting, and all pastimes which are useless,
degrading, a waste of time.

---

* At that time (4th century AD) the various public shows and sporting activities were often indecent : they were unsuitable for a child of God to take part in or be present at.

Cyril of Jerusalem

That is why the Christian asks God in prayer
to be released from fondness for these things.
We say to God :
Keep my eyes from what is false. Ps 118 (119).37

....

DO NOT SERVE THE SPIRIT OF EVIL

8 After that you say :
'I will not serve you, Spirit of Evil.'
To serve the spirit of evil
is to pray to false gods and honour lifeless idols,
to light lamps and burn incense near fountains and rivers.
Those who do this
are deceived by dreams of evil spirits :
they imagine they can cure their illnesses in this way.
You must not behave like this.
Consulting fortune-tellers, using charms, taking up magic,
all kinds of sorcery are ways of serving the Devil.
Don't have anything to do with them.

YOU HAVE CHOSEN TO FOLLOW CHRIST.
DO NOT LOOK BACK.

You have rejected Satan,
you belong to Christ.
So then if you fall back into Satan's wicked ways
you will discover him to be an even crueler
and harder taskmaster than before.
Previously,
the spirit of evil would have treated you as a friend,
making your slavery agreeable.
But now he will be angry with you.
And you will find yourself separated from Christ
and find the Devil very near you.

Cyril of Jerusalem

Surely you've heard what Scripture tells us
about Lot and his daughters ? Gen 19.15-26
Lot and his daughters were saved
because they fled into the mountains,
but his wife became a pillar of salt.
This happened because she wilfully disobeyed
and stopped to look back.
Let this be a warning to you.
Once you have begun a good work
do not look back at what the world is doing .....

9 So you have turned your back on Satan.
You completely cut the links you had with him.
And so there is nothing left to hold you in the land of death.
But the garden which God planted in the east
opens its gates to you.
Our first parent (Adam) was turned out of this garden
because he disobeyed God. Gen 3.23
You call all that to mind by turning from the west
to the east :
the east represents the light,
the direction from which the sun rises.
Then you were asked to say :
'I believe in the Father, the Son and the Holy Spirit,
and one baptism of repentance' —
things about which you were taught at some length
in your first instruction before baptism.

10 These words make you strong,
so be in earnest.
Yes, it is true as was just now read:
Our enemy the devil is like a lion :
he prowls around everywhere.

He is looking for someone to devour. 1 Pet 5.8
Indeed in former times death was completely victorious,
it devoured everything.
But with the washing of new birth (baptism)
God has wiped away all tears from every face. Rev 21.4
Now you have taken off your old clothing,
you have become a new person.
That is why you will no longer weep
but are enjoying a great celebration.
You have put on the garment of salvation
and this garment is Jesus Christ. Gal 3.27

11 That explains all that happened outside the baptistery.
God willing,
in the following instructions I shall give on the Sacraments,
we shall enter into the Holy of Holies. * 1 Kgs 8.6
Then we shall understand the reason
for all that takes place there.

Now, to God the Father with the Son and the Holy Spirit,
be glory and power and majesty for ever and ever.
Amen.

---

* The Holy of Holies was the most sacred part of the Temple of Solomon. There was kept the Ark of the Covenant, the sign of God's presence. In the Sacraments, God himself comes to us.

2

HOW TO UNDERSTAND YOUR BAPTISM
Romans 6.3-14

In this teaching session, Cyril recalls the actions which took place in the baptismal hall, and explains the meaning of each of these rites. He emphasises the way the Christian shares in the Passion of Christ which is at one and the same time death and life.

1 This fresh daily teaching on Baptism and the Eucharist
  is very useful for you,
  because it explains happenings still quite new to you.
  It is especially suitable for you because you have become
  new people,   Col 3.9-10
  and you have left your old way of life.
  That is why I must give you the continuation
  of yesterday's instruction.
  So you will understand the inner meaning
  of what happened in the Baptistery.

2 As soon as you came in, you took off your clothes.
  This action was a sign
  that you were leaving your former life-style.   *
  Without clothing you were naked and in this way
  you identified with Christ hanging on the cross.

---

* Col 3.9-10 : You have stripped off the old self with its practices.

Cyril of Jerusalem

> Without clothing you were naked
> and so you identified with Christ hanging on the cross.
> The naked Christ took away their strength from the spirits
> who held power and authority.
> Victor on the wood of the cross,
> Christ had them publicly displayed as prisoners
> in his victory parade.   Col 2.15
> Wicked spirits hid themselves in your body.
> That is why you may no longer wear those old clothes.
> I do not speak of the clothes we can see, but your former life
> when you were full of deceitful desires
> which were corrupting you.   Eph 4.22
> Anyone who gives up these old habits
> ought not to put them on again,
> but say with the spouse whom Christ has chosen :   *
> 'I have taken off my clothing.
> I am not going to put it on again.'   Song 5.3
> What a wonderful thing !
> You were absolutely naked in front of everyone
> and you were not ashamed.
> Yes, you were just like Adam the first man:
> in the Garden of Eden he was naked
> and was not ashamed.   Gen 2.25

3 Then, when you had taken off your clothing
> you were anointed with oil —
> from head to toe — with oil that had been blessed.   **
> So you were made ready to share in the life of Jesus Christ
> who is the true olive tree.   Rom 11.24

---

* Cyril is speaking here of the Beloved in the Song of Songs. She stands for both the Church and every Christian.

** This oil is not the symbol of the Holy Spirit but a pure olive oil used for the rite of purification.

The prayer over this oil gave it strength
to burn away all stain of sin
and send the evil spirits flying.

4 After this you were taken by the hand
and led to the baptismal bath.
In the same way they took Christ down from the cross
and placed him in the tomb,
the very tomb which is there before you. *
Then each one of you was asked :
' Do you believe
in the name of the Father, the Son and the Holy Spirit ? '
And you replied : 'Yes' : a 'yes' which brings salvation.
You were plunged three times under the water,
then you were brought out.
That serves to remind us
that Christ stayed three days in the tomb.
Our Saviour spent three days and three nights
in the belly of the earth.   Mt 12.40
When you were lifted up out of the water for the first time
you acted out the first day
on which Christ remained in the earth.
When you were plunged into the water,
that represented the night.
Indeed, during the night one no longer sees anything,
whereas during the day a person lives in the light.
In the same way, when you were plunged into the water
you could see nothing,
but when you came up out of the water,
you found yourself in the full light of day.
You died and were born in one and the same moment.
This saving water was both tomb and womb.

---

*   Cyril is speaking in front of Christ's Sepulchre in Jerusalem.

BAPTISM IS A NEW BIRTH

5 It is a strange thing, quite out of the ordinary.
For indeed, at the moment of Baptism
we are not actually dead,
we have not really been placed in the tomb,
we are not actually brought back from the dead :
by these ceremonies we seek to represent Christ's Passion .
Yet we are truly given new life.
Christ himself was actually nailed to a cross,
he was certainly buried in a tomb,
and he has truly risen again.
The benefits of his Passion are freely given to us :
so, by these ceremonies
we can share in the sufferings of Christ
and so we truly gain salvation.
Oh, yes, God's love for us is really immense.
Christ received the nails in his innocent hands and feet
and felt the pain and anguish.
As for me. I share in his Passion without pain or suffering
and Christ freely saves me.

BAPTISM MAKES US SHARERS IN THE PASSION OF CHRIST

6 Do not think then that Baptism only brings forgiveness of sins.
It also makes us children of God by adoption.
John's baptism gave only forgiveness of sins.
But we ourselves know quite well
that Baptism not only takes away sins
and allows us to receive the Holy Spirit.
It is also the counterpart of Christ's sufferings. *

---

* S. Cyril says : the antitype. To be baptised is to be made like Christ by spiritually but really taking part in his Passion, and so to be accepted by the Father as his child.

Cyril of Jerusalem

That is why Paul tells us quite plainly
in the reading we have just heard :
'Do you not know this ?
All of us who have been baptised into Christ Jesus
were baptised into his death.
Therefore we are buried with him
by Baptism into death.'   Rom 6.3-4
Paul probably spoke in this way because some believed
that baptism forgives sins
and makes us children of God by adoption,
but did not believe that baptism also makes us sharers
in the real sufferings of Christ
by carrying out the rites and ceremonies.

7 We must understand this :
everything that Christ endured
he suffered for us, to save us.
He did not pretend to suffer.
He felt all the pain and agony.
And we too share in his sufferings.
That is why Paul is right to say in all truth :
'We are completely united with Christ
in a death which is like his.
And so we shall rise from the dead
in a way which is like his resurrection. '   Rom 6.5

....

Pay close attention to the Apostle's words.
He did not say :
We are completely united with Christ through his death.
But rather :
We are united with him 'in a death like his.'
Yes, Christ really died.
The soul truly left his body

and he was truly buried in a tomb
and his sacred body was wrapped in pure linen.
All that truly happened for him.
For us, there is only the appearance
of the passion and death of Christ.
However, we are saved,
and that is not just an appearance, but a reality.

8 That's enough teaching for the moment. Don't forget it !
Then, unworthy as I am,
I can say to you what the apostle Paul said :
'I love you,
because you remember me always
and you keep the traditions
which I have handed on to you.' 1 Cor 11.2
God is all-powerful.
It is he who has brought you back to life
from the reign of death.
He can give you the grace
to walk in newness of life. Rom 6.13; 6.4
because his is the glory and the power, now and for ever.
Amen.

3

THE SIGNING WITH HOLY OIL REPRESENTS THE GIFT OF THE HOLY SPIRIT
1 John 2. 20-28

After baptism, the new Christian receives the Holy Spirit. This s what we call Confirmation. The Holy Spirit gives the Christian power to resist the attacks of the Spirit of Evil. n order to show clearly this giving of the Holy Spirit, the newly-baptised are anointed with oil mixed with perfume, on their eyes, forehead, mouth, nose and hands.

THE FATHER GAVE THE HOLY SPIRIT TO JESUS

1 You were baptised into Christ:
    you have put on Christ, *   Gal 3.27
    you have become conformed
    to the image of the Son of God.   Rom 8.29
    Indeed, God decided in advance
    to adopt you as his children.   Eph 1.5
    That is why he will make us
    like the glorious body of Christ.   Phil 3.21
    So now you have become followers of Christ

---

* The newly baptised wore a white garment during Easter Week to show clearly that now they belonged to Christ.

and they call you by that name, christs.   *
That is as it should be.
Truly, in one of the psalms God is talking about you
when he says :
'Do not touch my anointed ones.'   Ps 104 (105). 15
You have become anointed ones, other 'Christs',
when you received the sign of the Holy Spirit.
All this is brought about in you by imagery,
because you are images of Christ.

Christ bathed in the river Jordan.   Mt 3.13-17
By touching the waters
he gave them a share in his divine power.
When he came out of the water
the Holy Spirit actually rested upon him.
Like rested on like.   **
And you in the same way,
when you came out of the baptismal bath,
were also anointed with holy oil.
This oil represents the gift which Christ received,
that is to say the Holy Spirit.
Besides, the prophet Isaiah foretold all this.
He said in the person of Our Lord :
'The Spirit of the Lord is upon me.
That is why he has put his mark on me.
He has sent me
to bring good news to the poor.'   Is 61.1

---

*   Christs or anointed ones, signed with oil. Under the Old Covenant, priests and kings were anointed with oil to show that God chose them (greek Christos = latin Messiah = Anointed One) Under the new Covenant, the one whom God chooses is his Son, Jesus the Christ. Through our baptism and signing with the Holy Spirit, God chooses us also and makes us his sons and daughters in and through Jesus Christ.

**   The Spirit is God : the Son is God.

2 It was no one human who anointed Christ
with oil or any perfume made on earth.
But rather, God the Father chose him
and destined him to be the Saviour of the whole world
and anointed him with the Holy Spirit, as Peter says :
'Jesus of Nazareth
God anointed with the Holy Spirit.' Acts 10.38.
The prophet David also said :
'Your royal throne is established for ever.
You govern your kingdom with justice,
you love righteousness and hate wickedness.
That is why God has anointed you with the oil of gladness
and has singled you out
from your companions.' Ps 44(45).6-7

YOU ALSO RECEIVE THE HOLY SPIRIT

Christ really was nailed to the cross ;
he was buried in a tomb ;
he rose from the dead.
That experience is yours also,
but only by means of signs.
Through your baptism,
you were judged worthy to be nailed to the cross with Christ,
to be buried in the tomb,
and to rise from the dead with him.
It is the same for Confirmation.
Christ was anointed with the oil of gladness,
that is to say the Holy Spirit who gives spiritual gladness.
And you have been anointed with perfumed oil
and so you have become
companions and members of Christ. Rom 12.64,5

3 But pay attention !
Do not think that this perfumed oil is simply oil.

After the Holy Spirit is called upon in prayer
over the Eucharistic bread,
it is no longer simply bread,
but becomes the body of Christ.
In the same way, when we pray
that the Holy Spirit will come upon this perfumed oil,
it is no longer simply oil :
it becomes the gift of Christ. *
The Holy Spirit who is God is there, truly present.
He fills the oil with his power.
The sign of the cross is made on your eyes, your forehead,
your mouth, your nose and your hands
with this perfumed oil.
It is a sacrament (a sacred symbol) :
your body receives the oil which it can see,
but your whole soul becomes holy
through the holy unseen Spirit who gives life.

GOD GIVES YOU THE HOLY SPIRIT SO THAT YOU MAY RESIST THE EVIL ONE

4 First of all, your forehead is signed with the holy oil
to release you from shame.
Because of his disobedience,
Adam, the first man,
carried his shame with him everywhere.   Gen 3.7-10
And so, your face is unveiled
and the glory of the Lord
is reflected on you as in a mirror.   2 Cor 3.18
Then your ears are anointed :
and so you can listen
to the revelation of God's mysteries.

---

* Here, the gift of Christ is the Holy Spirit.

Cyril of Jerusalem

Isaiah said:
'The Lord has given me a listening ear.'   Is 50.4b,5
The Lord Jesus also says in the Gospel:
'Those who have ears let them listen.'   Mt 11.15
Then your nose is anointed
and so you smell the fragrance of the perfumed oil
and you can say:
'We are like a sweet-smelling perfume
which Christ offers to God.
This is the perfume of those God saves.'   2 Cor 2.15
After that your breast is signed with oil, and so you receive
the breastplate of righteousness,
and are able to resist
all the tricks of the Evil Spirit.   Eph 6.14 &11
After his baptism and the coming of the Holy Spirit,
Jesus, our Saviour,
went to fight the evil spirit in the desert.   Mk 4.1-10
In the same way, after Baptism and Confirmation,
God gives you, through the Holy Spirit,
all the help you need to fight evil.
You can now resist all attacks of the devil by saying:
'I can do all things
thanks to Christ who strengthens me.'   Phil 4.13

YOU ARE CALLED CHRISTIANS

5 You are considered worthy to be anointed with the holy oil
and then you are called Christians.
Because of your new birth you have a right to this name.
Before being considered worthy to receive Baptism
and the gift of the Holy Spirit,
you had no real right to the name.
But you were on the way
and were preparing to become Christians.

SYMBOLIC USE OF HOLY OIL IN THE OLD COVENANT

6 You ought to know this :
Under the Old Covenant already we find
rites using holy oil.   Lev 8.1-12
When Moses told his brother Aaron
what God had commanded
and when he made him high priest,
he bathed Aaron in water and anointed him with holy oil.
Because of this anointing,
they called Aaron : Christ (anointed one) .
It was a foreshadowing of greater things to come.
Similarly, when the high priest made Solomon king,
he anointed him with holy oil.
Beforehand, Solomon had bathed at Gihon.   1 Kgs 1.38-45
All these ceremonies
were preparation for what was to come.
For us these rites are no longer a preparation, no type,
but the reality.
Truly, Jesus Christ, the First-born,
was anointed with the Holy Spirit,
and it is through him that we are saved.
He was certainly offered first of all
and he is the first-fruits of that offering.
And you are the whole loaf offered to God.   Num 15.19-21
'If the first-fruits of bread is set aside for God,
then the whole loaf is consecrated to him also.'   Rom 11.16

LOOK AFTER THIS GIFT, DO NOT LET IT GET SOILED

7 Keep this gift unspotted..
It will teach you everything if it remains with you.
The apostle John says so in his first Letter,   1 Jn 2.27
which you have heard read out just now.

He has given many explanations
of the anointing with holy oil.
Truly, this gift cares for our body
through the power of the Holy Spirit
and has a saving effect on our whole person.
A long time ago,
 the prophet Isaiah foretold this when he said :
'And the Lord will make a feast for all peoples
on this mountain.' Is 25.6
This mountain stands for the Church.
Isaiah also speaks of the Church when he writes :
'In the last days,
the mountain of the Lord's house shall be established ;
they shall see from afar the mountain of the Lord.' Is 2.2
And again :
'They shall drink wine, they shall drink with joy.
They will be anointed with perfumed oil.' * Is 25.6,7
Isaiah wants you to understand
the real meaning of this oil which is not an earthly one.
He says : ' Tell this to all the other nations,
because this plan of the Lord's is for everyone.' Is 25.7

So now, you have been anointed with this oil,
the sign of the Holy Spirit.
Guard it with great care : do not allow it to be soiled.
Make progress in good works
and look for ways of pleasing the Master
who is leading us to salvation,
Jesus Christ.
To Him be the glory, for ever and ever.   Amen.

---

* Taken from the Greek version, called the Septuagint.

Cyril of Jerusalem

4

YOU RECEIVE
THE BODY AND BLOOD OF CHRIST
1 Corinthians 11. 23 - 25

After Baptism and Confirmation, the new Christians receive the Eucharist (Holy Communion)

WE ARE CHRIST-BEARERS   GAL 2.20

1 The teaching of the apostle Paul
 is quite enough to establish our faith in the Eucharist.
 You were considered ready to receive Communion
 and so you have become as one
 with the Body and Blood of Jesus Christ.   Eph 3.6
 the apostle Paul states quite clearly :   1 Cor 11.23-25
     On the night he was betrayed our Lord Jesus Christ
    took bread, and gave thanks to God.
 Then he broke the bread and gave it to his disciples saying :
           — Take, eat :
             this is my body. —
            Then he took a cup of wine.
            He thanked God and said :
           — Take, drink :
            this is my blood. —

So, when Jesus himself states solemnly about the bread :
" This is my body "
can anyone still ask if it is true ?

Cyril of Jerusalem

And when he says clearly:
" This is my blood "
can anyone still doubt and say : 'No, it is not his blood' ?

2 On a previous occasion, at Cana in Galilee,
Jesus changed water into wine
because it pleased him to do so.
How then can one not believe it
when he changes wine into his Blood ?
He was invited to an earthly marriage
and he worked an astonishing miracle.
So then, when he gives to the Bridegroom's friends, *
to the children of God,
the gift of his Body and Blood,
how can we not believe that this also is true ?

3 We are completely sure of this :
It is the body and Blood of Christ that we receive.
True, you are given something which looks like bread,
but it is certainly
the Body of Christ that you receive.
You are given a drink that looks like wine,
but it is truly the Blood of Cbrist which you receive.
So, when you have received
the Body and Blood of Christ,
you become totally united with him.
So we become 'Christ-bearers'.
His Body and Blood
become part of our bodies.
In this way, as the apostle Peter expresses it :
We become sharers
in the nature of God himself. 2 Pet 1.4

---

* The Bridegroom's friends are Christ's followers. The Bridegroom is Christ himself. The Church is his Bride. see Mt 9.15

BREAD THE BODY OF CHRIST.
WINE THE BLOOD OF CHRIST

4 Previously Christ had said to the Jews :
If you do not eat my body, if you do not drink my blood,
you can have no life in you.   Jn 6.53
the Jews did not understand him spiritually.
They took offence and walked away from Jesus.
There is no doubt they believed that the Saviour
was inviting them to eat his physical body.   Jn 6.61-66

....

6 Do not consider the Bread and Wine to be
ordinary bread and wine.
This bread is the Body of Christ,
this wine is the Blood of Christ :
the Lord himself said so.
It is true, you see bread and wine,
but let your faith remove your doubt.
Do not judge by what they taste like.
Go on firmly believing
that you have been allowed to receive
the Body and Blood of Christ.

....

9 You have been instructed,
and this is what you must firmly believe :
What appears to be bread, is not bread.
It tastes like bread but it is the Body of Christ.
What appears to be wine is not wine —
even though as you taste it you could think so —
but the Blood of Christ.

Cyril of Jerusalem

You know also what David said long ago in a psalm :
Bread gives strength to human beings,
and thanks to oil their faces shine with joy. Ps 103(104).15
Make your heart strong
by eating this spiritual bread,
and make your soul shine with joy.
May your soul be unveiled
because you have a clear conscience.
Then the glory of the Lord will be reflected on you
as in a mirror,
and you will change from glory into glory, 2 Cor 3.18
united to Christ Jesus our Lord.

To him be honour and might and glory
        for ever and ever.
                Amen.

5

SEE HOW THE EUCHARIST IS CELEBRATED
1 Peter 2.1

At a final meeting Cyril explains the different parts of the Eucharistic Celebration (Mass), because the catechumens were not present for this celebration before their baptism. They had to leave the church after the readings and sermon, so the celebration of the Eucharistic Liturgy is a new experience for them.

1. With the help of our loving God
   I have spoken a lot to you at earlier meetings
   about Baptism, the gift of the Holy Spirit *
   and the Eucharist.
   Now it is time to pass on to what is next.
   Today I must bring your catechesis (instruction) to an end.

THE PRIESTS WASH THEIR HANDS — WHY IS THIS ?

2. You've seen what happens :
   the deacon offers water to the bishop
   and the other priests who are standing at the altar.
   Then they wash their hands.
   The deacon doesn't give water because their hands are dirty.
   We had clean hands when we came into the church
   at the beginning of Mass.

---

* The gift of the Holy Spirit is the Sacrament of Confirmation. See Instruction 3 p 51

Cyril of Jerusalem

The washing of hands is a sign
that we must be pure in heart.
We must free ourselves of all our faults and sins.
Hands are a symbol of our actions.
So in washing them we symbolise
that our actions are pure and blameless.
Do you remember, David explained this mystery
when he said in a psalm :
O Lord, I will wash my hands among the innocent
and go around your altar.   Ps 25 (26).6
So, washing our hands shows
that we want to free ourselves from sin.

THE SIGN OF PEACE

3 Then the deacon says in a loud voice :
'Let us embrace each other.'
Do not think that this gesture is like the one we use
to greet a friend in the street.
It is not at all the same.
Rather, this gesture unites people's hearts
and seeks entire forgiveness.
It is the sign that their hearts are as one
and that they dismiss all bad feeling.
That is why Christ said :
" When you come to make an offering to God,
if at that moment you remember
that your brother has something against you,
then leave your offering in front of the altar
and go straight away to make peace with your brother.
Then come and present your offering to God. "   Mt 5.23-24
This kiss of peace is, then, a proof of reconciliation.
It is called a holy kiss.
The apostle Paul says clearly in his letters :
'Greet each other with a holy kiss.'   Rom 16.16; 1 Cor 16.20

Cyril of Jerusalem

And the apostle Peter writes :
'Greet each other with a kiss of love.' 1 Pet 5.14

PREPARATION FOR THE PRAYER OF PRAISE (EUCHARISTIC PRAYER)

4 After that, the Bishop then said in a loud voice :
" Lift up your hearts."
Indeed, at this solemn moment
we should certainly lift up our hearts to God,
and not be thinking about earthly things
and day-to-day matters.
The Bishop was urging everybody at this moment
to forget about their worries, their family cares,
and to turn their hearts to heaven,
towards God who loves us.
So you replied :
" We lift them up to the Lord."
Now, in saying these words,
you show you are in agreement with him.
It's no use your lips saying :
'We lift them up to the Lord'
when at the same time your mind is busy with life's cares.
Certainly, we should be thinking about God at all times,
but that's impossible because of our human weakness.
However, at this moment above all,
we should make every effort to do so.

5 Then the Bishop said :
" Let us give thanks to the Lord our God."
Yes, truly we ought to thank God :
we were not worthy of him,
yet he has called us to receive such a wonderful gift.
We were God's enemies
and he has reconciled us to himself. Rom 5.10

Cyril of Jerusalem

He considered us worthy to receive the Holy Spirit
which makes us children of God. Rom 8.14
So you respond :
" It is right and fitting."
When we thank God
we are doing what is right and fitting.
Our Lord himself not only did what is fitting
but he went much further than what is merely fitting.
He did what benefited us too
and thought us worthy of such great gifts.

THE PRAYER OF PRAISE

6 After that, we recall all that God has created :
the land, the sea, the sun, moon and stars,
all rational beings and those without reason,
beings we can see and those we cannot see,
all the ranks of God's angels .....
' Proclaim the Lord's greatness with me.' Ps 33 (34).3
We are reminded of the seraphim. Is 6.2-3
Inspired by the Holy Spirit,
Isaiah had a vision of them forming a circle around God,
the great King.
They hid their faces with two wings,
their feet with two more wings,
and with a third pair they flew, and they cried out :
' Holy, holy, holy is the Lord, God of the universe.'
That is why, to praise God,
we say this prayer which the seraphim taught us.
And in this way, we share in the song of the angels
in heaven.

ASKING THE HELP OF THE HOLY SPIRIT (EPICLESIS)

7 Sanctifying ourselves with these spiritual hymns,
we can then ask of God who loves us :

Cyril of Jerusalem

'Send your Holy Spirit upon these gifts (on the altar),
that they may become the body and blood
of our Lord Jesus Christ.'
Indeed, all that the Holy Spirit touches becomes holy
and is transformed.

PRAYER FOR THE LIVING

8 This sacrifice in which there is no blood poured out
has been offered, then, through the power of the Holy Spirit.
We next ask God to look upon Christ
who is himself offered in sacrifice.
We pray for the peace of all the Churches,
for peace in the world,
for heads of state, for their armies and their allies,
for the sick and those who are in difficulties of any kind.
In a word : for all.
We pray for all in need of help
and we offer for them the sacrifice of Christ.

PRAYER FOR THE DEAD

9 Then we remember also those who have died.
First of all,
friends of God who lived holy lives before Christ came,
prophets, apostles, martyrs.
With the help of their prayers
we hope that God will answer ours.
Next we pray for the Fathers of the Church, the Bishops,
and those of our community who have gone before us.
We believe that our prayers will be very helpful to all,
mainly because Christ, himself the most sacred offering,
is actually present on the altar.

10 What I say is true. An example will make it clear to you.
I do know that a good many people say this :

Cyril of Jerusalem

'To pray during the offering of the Mass (Eucharist)
for someone who died, with or without sins,
what good does that do anyone ?'
Consider this :
   A king sends into exile
   his servants who have plotted against him.
   But the friends of these servants
   prepare a splendid present, and they take it to the king
   to persuade him to accept it
   and grant pardon to the servants being punished.
   The king will surely be moved
   to cancel the sentence on those disloyal servants.
In the same way, we too
pray to God for the dead, even for sinners.
We do not have a present to offer God
but we offer Jesus Christ who died on the cross for our sins.
And so we obtain forgiveness for them and for ourselves
from our God who loves us.

THE OUR FATHER

11 After that, you say this prayer
    which the Saviour gave to his disciples.
    With a pure heart you give to God the name of Father,
    and you say :
    'Our Father who are in heaven.'   Mt 6.9
    How great is God's love for us !
    We had turned our backs on him,
    we were miserable sinners.
    And God has completely forgiven all our sins.
    He loved us so much that we call him : Father.
    'Our Father who are in heaven ' .....

12 ' Hallowed be your Name.'
    God's Name is always holy

whether we say so or not.
But sometimes there are sinful people who insult his Name.
As we read in the Bible :
'Because of you
my name is insulted among the gentiles.'   *   Is 52.5; Rom 2.24
So we ask
that the name of God may become holy and honoured in us.
This Name is already holy before we ask :
it does not have to become so.
But it becomes holy in us
when we become holy ourselves,
when our actions are worthy of Christians.

13 ' Your kingdom come.'
One needs a pure heart to say with boldness :
Your kingdom come.
You have heard the apostle Paul say :
'Sin must no longer reign
in your mortal bodies.'   Rom 6.12
So, if you have purified your actions, thoughts and words
you can say to God :
Your kingdom come.

14 ' Your will be done as it is in heaven.'
The holy and blessed angels of God obey his will.
David says :
'All you angels, bless the Lord,
mighty in power,
fulfilling his word.'   Ps 133 (134). 10
So you mean by this prayer :
Like the angels in heaven who do your will
may I even on earth also do your will, Lord.

---

*   Isaiah is speaking to the People of Israel : the gentiles are non-Jews

15 'Give us this day our life-giving bread' *
   Ordinary bread is not the life-giving bread.
   Life-giving bread is for our soul as well as our body .....
   By 'this day' he means 'each day'
   as St Paul has said : 'While it is still called today.'   Heb 3.13

16 'And forgive us our sins,
   as we forgive those who sin against us.'
   Indeed we are far from perfect,
   and we sin in our words and thoughts.
   Many of our actions also are worthy of blame.
   The apostle John says :
   'If we say we are without sin,
   we are liars.'   1 Jn 1.8

   We make an agreement with God :
   we ask him to forgive our sins
   as we forgive our neighbours who offend against us.
   Consider what we receive from God
   in exchange for what we give !
   So without waiting or leaving it till much later,
   let us forgive each other.
   The sins which others commit against us
   are slight, unimportant, and easy to forgive.
   But those which we commit against God are serious
   and only his great love can blot them out.
   Be warned then,
   or your failure to forgive simple offences against yourself
   will prevent you from receiving from God
   forgiveness for your own very serious sins against him .....

---

* This bread is the Body of Christ.

17 'And lead us not into temptation, Lord.'
Is the Lord advising us to ask not to be tempted at all ?
And yet it says in Scripture :
'One who has not been tested
has not given proof of his intentions.'   Sir 34.10
And again :
'Be very happy, my brothers and sisters,
when you meet trials of all kinds.'   Jas 1.2
The meaning is that being tempted or tested
is not the same thing
as being overcome by temptation.
Temptation, it seems, is like a river in flood,
difficult to cross.
Some people do not drown in this torrent of temptation.
They swim very strongly and pass through it
without letting it carry them away.
On the other hand,
others who do not possess the same qualities
enter the torrent of temptation and are drowned by it.
For example :
Judas was tempted by his great love of money.
He did not know how to steer his way through the temptation.
In fact it swept over him
and took up his whole being, body and soul,
and covered him.
Peter also was tempted and he said :
'I do not know Jesus.'
He gave way to that temptation,
but it did not overpower him completely.
He steered his way through it with courage
and he was able to escape.
In another place in the Scriptures, listen then
to the friends of God who won their victory over temptation.

Cyril of Jerusalem

They thank God for freeing them from temptation, saying :
' God, you put us to the test.
You have made us pass through fire,
as silver is tried by fire.
You have made us fall into a snare.
On our backs you have placed heavy burdens.
You have put men over our heads.
We have had to pass through fire and water
but you have brought us out in peace.   Ps 65 (66).10-12
As you see, they spoke out boldly
because they passed through temptation
and were not drowned by it.
'You have brought us out in peace ' :
to be brought out in peace means
to escape from temptation.

18 'But deliver us from evil.'
If that meant the same as :
And lead us not into temptation,
Our Lord would not have said : But deliver us from evil.
Evil is our enemy, the Spirit of Evil,
and we ask to be delivered from it.

Then at the end of the prayer you say: : 'Amen.'
By this amen, which means 'let it be so'
you show your agreement with all the words of this prayer
which the Lord taught us.

YOU RECEIVE THE BODY AND BLOOD OF CHRIST

19 After that, the Bishop said :
"Holy things for holy people."
The holy things are the Body and Blood placed on the altar
because the Holy Spirit has come upon them.
But you too are holy

because you have become worthy to receive the Holy Spirit.
And so the holy things and holy people are united.
Then you said :
'There is only one who is holy, our Saviour, Jesus Christ.'
Yes, that's true, there is only One who is holy,
holy that is in himself.
But we too are holy, though not by nature.
We become holy only by sharing in the life of Christ,
and making an effort to change our life,
and by prayer.

20 After this, you heard the voice of the cantor.
He invited you to share in the holy mysteries (the Eucharist).
For this he sings in a melody worthy of God :
'Taste and see
that the Lord is good.'   Ps 33 (34).9
Do not judge according to what you taste,
but according to what you believe.
For in tasting,
it is not bread and wine that we are asked to recognise
but the Body and Blood of Christ
under the appearances of bread and wine.

21 When you come forward
do not approach with hands wide apart in front of you.
Do not spread out you fingers, either.
But make with your left hand a royal throne for your right,
for this hand must be ready to receive the King.
You receive the Body of Christ in the hollow of your hand
and you say : 'Amen'.
Then carefully hold this most holy Body to your eyes
and your eyes will become holy too.
Then receive the Body of Christ
and be sure not to lose even the smallest crumb.

Because, if you lose even the smallest fragment
it is as if you lose part of your own body.
Tell me truly :
If you were given some small pieces of gold
you would look after them most carefully,
you would make sure not to lose any, wouldn't you ?
If you did, it would be a cause of unhappiness for you.
Should you not, then,
be much more careful with the Body of Christ ?
Christ's Body is more precious than gold or precious stones.
So be very careful not to lose the least little bit.

22 Then, after you have received the Body of Christ
you come to drink from the Cup of his Blood.
Do not stretch out your hands
but bow your head and, with love and reverence,
say : Amen.
And become holy by receiving the Blood of Christ also.
While your lips are still moist
gently touch them with your fingers.
Then touch your eyes, your forehead and other sense organs
to make them holy too.
Then while waiting for the prayer to be said
thank God who considered you worthy
to receive such wonderful sacraments.

FINAL WORD OF ADVICE

23 Keep to these traditions. Do not change anything .
And as for yourselves, remain pure in heart.
Do not cut yourself off from Communion,
do not let sin distance you from these most holy sacraments.
May the God of peace make you completely holy.

May he keep your spirit, soul and body pure
without trace of sin
until the coming of our Lord Jesus Christ.   1 Thess 5.23

> To him be glory and honour and power,
>   with the Father and the Holy Spirit,
>   now and for ever
>   and world without end.
>   Amen.

AUGUSTINE OF HIPPO

Easter Sermons

- **SERMON 211** 77
WE MUST LOVE AND FORGIVE

- **SERMON 212** 88
THE 'I BELIEVE'

- **SERMON 59** 95
THE 'OUR FATHER

-**SERMON GUELFERBYTANUS** 104
THE LORD'S PASSION

-**SERMON 227** 108
THE EUCHARIST

-**SERMON 232** 114
THE RESURRECTION

Sermon 211

WE MUST LOVE AND FORGIVE

It is the beginning of Lent. Augustine is speaking to his people and to those preparing for baptism. He wants them to learn to live in peace and to forgive. For this purpose he gives them some examples.

FORGIVE YOUR BROTHER AND SISTERS AND GOD WILL FORGIVE YOU

1 Lent is a time reserved for God.
  That is why I wish to speak to you
  about understanding the peaceful relationship
  which must exist between Christian brothers and sisters.
  So, if someone has a quarrel with another person
  he must end it before it makes an end of him !
  My brothers, what I am saying to you is serious.
  On this earth, the difficulties that we meet
  are a danger for our weak life,
  which ends in death.
  It is necessary to pray to God
  so that these difficulties do not drown us.
  Even a good person sins in some way.
  That is why God our Master teaches us to say
  in the Lord's Prayer:
  'Forgive us our wrong-doing
  as we forgive those who do wrong to us.' Mt 6.12

It is the only remedy which gives life.
We make an agreement with God
and offer our forgiveness as security
We ask God with great confidence:
"Forgive us our sins".
And we agree to one condition:
we must also forgive
those who have offended us.
If we do not forgive others,
do not think that God will forgive us our sins.
Do not deceive yourselves:
God does not deceive anyone.

Do not be angry.

We easily become angry. It is human.
If only we could not get angry !
It is human to get angry
but it is not necessary that your anger becomes very strong.
At first it is a little shoot
but it must not grow big, watered by suspicions.
It must not become a great tree-trunk of hate.
Anger is one thing, hatred is another thing.
Take an example:
A father is angry with his son. It often happens.
But the father does not hate his son.
He is angry in order to correct him.
It is because of love for his son that he is angry.
In the Gospel indeed we read:
'You see the little bit of wood in your brother's eye
but you do not see the tree-trunk in your own.'   Mt 7.3
You blame your brother when he is angry
and you keep hatred in your own heart.
In comparison with hatred
anger is a small shoot.

But if you feed the shoot it will become a tree.
If you root it out, it will be nothing.

IF YOU HATE YOUR BROTHER YOU ARE IN A DARK PRISON

2 When you heard the letter of St John,
if you listened well you should be afraid.
For this is what it says:
'The darkness is near its end
and already the true light is shining.' 1 Jn 2.8
And again:
'If someone says: "I am in the light"
and hates a brother or sister,
that one is still in the darkness.' 1 Jn 2.9
Perhaps you think
it is darkness like prisoners have to suffer in their prison.
If only it was that sort of darkness!
Nobody wants to live in darkness like that,
yet innocent people are sometimes shut away
in the darkness of prisons.
And the martyrs are shut in that darkness.
Around them was deep darkness
but light shone in their hearts. Ps 36(35). 9
In the night of their prison they could not see,
but because of the love they had for their brothers
they saw God.
The Apostle John writes:
Anyone who hates a brother or sister
is still in darkness. 1 Jn 2.9
In another place John writes:
'One who hates a brother or sister is a murderer.' 1 Jn 3.15
One who hates his brother walks freely,
he goes in and out, he goes away.

He is not in chains,
he is not in prison.
But his crime binds him.
Do not think: No, he is not in prison.
Be sure it is his heart which is his prison.
When you hear:
'The one who hates brother or sister is still in darkness'
do not believe that it is a small matter.
For the Apostle also says:
'The one who hates is a murderer.'
You hate your brother or your sister.
And you walk about without anxiety.
You do not want to make peace.
Do you not realise that God is allowing you time for that?
You have become a murderer and you still live.
If God was angry with you
you would die immediately
with a heart full of bad feelings
against your brother or your sister.
But God shows you mercy.
You too, then, must show mercy to yourself:
be at peace with your brother.

Your brother or sister does not want to make peace

But perhaps you want to be at peace
and your brother does not want to be?
It is enough for you to want to make peace.
You are now free.
You can be sorry for him.
If you want to make peace and your brother does not,
say without fear:
"Forgive us our offences
as we forgive those who have offended us."

Augustine

3 Suppose that you have done wrong to your brother.
Afterwards you want to make peace with him.
You want to say to him:
"Brother, forgive me, I have done you wrong"
but he does not forgive you, he will not wipe out your debt,
he will not forget the wrong you have done him.
He must watch out, when he goes to pray !
He goes to pray
and he has not forgiven the wrong you have done.
What is it that he must say in his prayer ?
He must say:
"Our Father in heaven." Mt 6.9-12
So he says that. Next comes:
"May your name be held holy."
After that:
"May your kingdom come."
Then it goes on:
"May your will be done on earth as it is in heaven."
What next ?
"Give us this day our daily bread."
That is as far as he can go.

See now, you who do not want to forgive,
do you perhaps want to go on to what follows ?
You are not able to continue.
You have stopped yourself there.
Yet if you must continue then speak the truth.
If you have no reason to say 'forgive us our sins'
then, do not say so.
But what do you think of what the Apostle John said:
'If we say we have no sin we mislead ourselves
and the truth is not in us.' 1 Jn 1.8
If your conscience pricks because you have been weak
(and on this earth there is plenty of evil everywhere)

Augustine

then say: "Forgive us our offences."
But see what follows.
You did not want to forgive your brother
and you want to say:
"As we forgive those who have offended us."
Are you going to say those words ?
But, if you are not going to say them
you will not receive any forgiveness.
And if you say them, you speak an untruth.
How will you speak the truth,
if you will not excuse your brother for his fault ?

God will grant you his pardon

4 I have warned you.
Now, I come to comfort you, whoever you are,
if only you say to your brother or sister:
"Forgive me the wrong I have done to you."
If you have said it with all your heart, truly and humbly,
with sincere love
God sees the depth of your heart,
he knows that you are speaking the truth.
But your brother does not want to forgive your fault.
Do not be anxious, then.
Both of you are God's servants and you have one Father.
You have wronged your companion
and he does not want to forgive.
Tell God about it. He is your master and his.
The Master will give you his forgiveness.
Your companion will not be able to demand anything more.

So I have warned the one who does not want to forgive
when the other asks him.
He must do what he does not want
or when he prays he will not receive what he wants.

And I have advised the one
who asked his brother's pardon for his fault
and did not receive pardon
that he can be sure of receiving from God
what he did not get from his brother.

RECOGNISE YOUR FAULTS.

Again, another piece of advice....
Your brother has done you wrong
and he does not want to say to you:
"I have done you harm, forgive me."
That kind of fault grows like weeds:
may God clear them out of his field,
that is to say, out of your hearts.
For there are many people
who know they have done wrong to their brothers
and they do not want to say: "Forgive me."
They were not ashamed to do what they did
but they are ashamed to ask pardon.
They were not ashamed of doing wrong
but they are ashamed to be humble.

Among us there are those
who are not in agreement with their brothers.
It is to you first that I am speaking
and calling you back to yourselves.
Consider and pass just judgment on yourselves.
Reflect within you and you will find:
'I ought not to have done what I did.
I ought not to have said what I said.'
So then, brother, ask pardon from your brothers.
Do to others what the Apostle Paul asks:
'Forgive one another
as God in Christ has forgiven you.' Eph 4.32

ASK PARDON OF YOUR BROTHERS AND SISTERS
WHILE YOU STILL HAVE LIFE

I say the same to all, men and women,
young and old, ordinary people and ministers of the Church,
and I say it also to myself.
We must all listen, we must all fear.
If we have done wrong to our brothers and sisters
and God still allows us to live
and we are not yet judged,
then, while we live,
we must do what our Father commands us.
He will be our judge.
If we have done something wrong to our brother or sister,
if we have done something to hurt them,
then we must ask their pardon....

Sometimes a master does wrong to one who works for him.
He is the master but both are God's servants.
Both have been saved by Christ's blood.
However hard it seems I still say
 that if a master has perhaps done something unjust,
he must say to the other: "Forgive me, pardon me"
or at least speak to him in a friendly way
and ask God's forgiveness.
To speak in a friendly way is to ask pardon....

MUST YOU ASK PARDON
WHEN YOU HAVE NOT DONE ANY HARM ?

5 Now I say to you all: We are beginning the holy days.
Take care that there is no disagreement among you.
I think some among you look into the depth of your heart
 and know you are not always in agreement with each other.

You find that you have not done wrong
but your brothers have hurt you....
Perhaps you are saying to yourselves:
"I want to make peace
but it is my brother who has insulted me.
It is he who has done wrong
and he will not say that he is sorry."
What am I going to say ?
'Go to your brother and say that you are sorry' ?
No, surely not. I do not want you to lie.
I do not want you to say to your brother:
'Forgive me'
when you know you have done no wrong.
What use is it to you to accuse yourself ?
You have not insulted your brother,
you have done him no wrong.
So why do you ask his pardon ?
That will do you no good. I do not want you to do that.

ASK THE HELP OF FRIENDS WHO LOVE PEACE

You know and you are sure, you have reflected well:
it is your brother who has done you harm
and you have done nothing to him ?
You answer: 'I am sure.'
Let this consciousness you have
be your conscience.
Therefore do not go to your brother
if it is he who has done you wrong. Do not ask forgiveness.

But surely there are among you
some of the brothers who love peace.
They will act as an intermediary between you.
They will speak to the brother who has harmed you.
They will urge him to ask your forgiveness..

Augustine

First ask forgiveness of God,
and be ready to forgive.
Be absolutely ready to pardon him with all your heart.
If you are ready to forgive him,
then you are forgiven.

THERE MUST BE PRAYER

For this, you have to pray.
Pray for your brother that he will ask your pardon.
You know it will harm him if he does not ask forgiveness,
so pray for him so that he does....
In your prayer, say to the Lord: "Lord, you know it all.
You know I have not wronged my brother.
It is he who has wronged me.
It is not good for him if he does not ask my pardon.
And so, Lord, I ask you sincerely to forgive him."

IMITATE THE LORD JESUS

Now I have told you what you, and I, should do,
especially during this time of Lent.
During Lent you fast, you pray and go to church more,
you do not want to please your body.
And you should be in harmony
with your brothers and sisters.
I am happy and I rejoice that you are in peace.
I do not want you to quarrel.
Yes, 'bear with one another
if anyone has a complaint against another.' Col 3.13
Then we shall celebrate the holy days of Easter in peace.
In peace we shall celebrate
the Passion of our Lord Jesus Christ.
He owed nothing to anyone.
Yet he paid back the debt of those who ought to have paid.

I tell you, the Lord Jesus Christ did not wrong anyone.
The whole world did wrong to him
and he did not demand punishment,
but promised a reward.
So we have him as a witness to our hearts:
if we have done wrong to someone
we ask pardon with all our heart.
And if someone has done wrong to us
we are ready to give our pardon
and we pray for our enemies.

Brothers, do not desire to return evil for evil.
What is revenge ?
It is to feed upon another's misfortune....
I know people say: 'Lord, give me revenge, kill my enemy'.
Pray honestly, for the enemy to be killed *
and your brother saved !
Pray for the hatred to be killed,
human nature to be saved.
Do pray that God may give you this vengeance:
let the one who treated you badly die
and be given back to you as a friend.

---

* Here St Augustine is reminding us that we should hate sin and love the sinner.

Sermon 212
THE 'I BELIEVE'

This is a very important instruction in Christian initiation. Fifteen days before Easter, the text of the Creed: 'I believe in God', is given to the catechumens. Then some days later, in the course of a ceremony, they will say it.

On the night of Holy Saturday they say it to all the assembly: it is their promise and their commitment. So, in the church before the people, the baptised Christians, they bind themselves to be true followers of Jesus Christ.

Augustine here presents this text. It contains all a Christian must believe.

1 Now the time has come
when you are going to receive a brief account
of what you must believe in order to be saved.
We call it 'The Symbol'.
This word 'symbol' comes from the Greek language.
It means a sign.
When merchants make a business deal between them,
they give each other a sign to show that they have agreed.
That sign is called a 'symbol'.
It is a mark of the contract which unites these merchants,
and it obliges them to be faithful in their agreement.
Your group of catechumens is a business group
dealing in the things of the Spirit.
You are like merchants

who search for a beautiful pearl.   Mt 13.45
That pearl is love.
God pours his love into our hearts
by the Holy Spirit, whom he will give to you.   Rom 5.5
That love you receive through your faith, *
and what you must believe is said in the 'I believe in God'.

THE FATHER IS GOD

To have faith
is to believe in God, the Father Almighty.
We cannot see him, he is invisible..
He does not die, he is everlasting.
He is the King of all ages.
He created all things, seen and unseen.

THE SON IS GOD

You do not separate the Son and God the Most High.
What you say of the Father
you are able to say of the Son also.
Indeed, the Son has said:
"The Father and I, we are one."   Jn 10.30
The Apostle Paul also wrote: 'The Son is in very nature God.
He is equal to the Father
and that equality is not a robbery.'   Phil 2.6
Indeed, to rob is to take what belongs to another.
But the Son is equal to the Father. It is his nature.
Is the Son almighty ?
Yes, 'through him all things were made'   Jn 1.3
More, 'He is the power of God
and the wisdom of God'   1 Cor 1.2
About him it is written:
'That wisdom is but one, yet it can do all things.'   Wis 7.27

---

* This faith is trust and belief in God

Augustine

In all that God is, the Son is equal to the Father.
He is, then, invisible since he is in the Father.
Indeed the Word of the Father, that is to say, the Son
is from the beginning with God,
and that Word is God. Jn 1.1
Moreover, since he is God,
the Son does not die. He lives for ever.
He is always the same, he does not change.

The human soul does not die
but it changes and can weaken or progress.
So its death is to be apart from the life of God
through ignorance of what it is ;
but its life is to run to the fountain of life
so that in God's light it may see light. Ps 36(35).9
This life will be for you too in the grace of Christ
for you will have life when you renounce that death. *

The Word of the Father is the only Son of God.
He lives with the Father.
That life is changeless, it cannot weaken nor progress.
What is permanent cannot grow less.
What is perfect cannot grow more perfect.
The Son is the creator of things seen and unseen.
Yes, the Apostle Paul has said:
'All things were created in the Son,
in heaven and on earth.
He has created all things seen and unseen
and heavenly powers
and any spirits with authority and power in the world.
All things are created by the Son and for the Son,
and in him all things hold together.' Col 1.16-17

---

* In these lines, St Augustine is speaking of Baptism.

THE SON WAS MADE MAN

But all that the Son of God has,
he left.
Always remaining God,
he became a servant. Phil 2.7
The One who is unseen
has become seen
because he took the state of a servant:
— he was born of the Holy Spirit and the Virgin Mary.
In that state of a servant,
he who is almighty
became weak.
— he suffered under Pontius Pilate.
As a servant
he who lives for ever
could die.
— he was nailed to the cross and buried.
In that state of a servant,
Creator of all things seen and unseen,
— he ascended into heaven,
which he had never left.
In that state of a servant,
— he sits at the right of the Father.
It is about this that the Prophet says:
'To whom has the arm of the Lord been revealed ?' Is 53.1
— he will come to judge the living and the dead.
In that state of a servant
he willed to die like us all,
he who is the life of the living.

THE HOLY SPIRIT IS GOD

Through the Son, the Father has sent us the Holy Spirit.
The Holy Spirit is the Spirit of the Father and of the Son.

They both send him
but he is not born of either of them.
That Spirit is one with them both.
He is equal to them both.

IN GOD THERE ARE THREE PERSONS:
THE FATHER, THE SON AND THE HOLY SPIRIT

The Father, the Son, and the Holy Spirit are the Trinity,
one God,
all-powerful, invisible,
King of all ages, Creator of all things seen and unseen.
We do not say::
there are three Gods, three who are all-powerful,
three creators.
We do not speak like that at all about God.
There are not three Gods,
but one God.
Although in the Trinity, Father, Son and Holy Spirit,
the Father is not the Son,
the Son is not the Father, and the Holy Spirit
is neither the Father nor the Son,
yet the Father of the Son is one,
the Son of the Father is one,
and the Spirit of the Father and of the Son is one.

Believe in order to understand.
For if you will not believe you will not understand.   Is 7.9

FAITH WILL SAVE YOU

If you believe,
then hope for grace.
In that grace, God will pardon all your sins.
For in that grace you will be saved;
not by yourselves, for it is the gift of God.   Eph 2.8-9

Augustine

All humans have to die
because of the fault of the first man,   1 Cor 21-22
and it is right and just.
But after death, at the end of time,
hope also that your body will be raised from death.
Death comes to everyone
because of the fault of the first human being,
but not everyone rises to the sufferings of the wicked.
Nor, as the foolish think,
do we rise to the joys of fleshly desires.
It will be as the Apostle says:
'It is sown a natural body,
it is raised a spirit body.'   1 Cor 15.44
So it will not then be a weight upon the soul,   Wis 9.15
nor will it need any food
because it will not suffer any weakness.

2 Now I have given you the whole Creed
gathered into this short talk.
I do not mean that you should write the words
but you should keep them in your memory
and recall them.
All that you have heard in the 'I believe'
is contained in the words of the Holy Bible.
But what I have told you briefly
will be a covenant for you according to God's promise
where, in the words of the prophet,
he speaks of the New Testament:
'This is the covenant which I will make after those days, *
says the Lord,
when I will put my law in their minds
and I will write it upon their hearts.'   Jer 31.33

---

* A covenant is a solemn agreement, and especially God' promise in the Old and New Testaments.

Praise him who has called you to glory, in his Kingdom.
His grace has brought you new life
and he will write the 'Symbol' in your hearts
through his Holy Spirit.
Then you will love what you believe
and faith will act in you through love.
Then you will please the Lord God,
who gives everything that is good.
You will not act as slaves
who are afraid of being punished,
but as free persons
who love the God who saves you.

This then is the 'Symbol', the Creed, the 'I believe in God'.
You will read about it in the Bible
and hear about it in church.
This short form 'I believe in God'
will help you to remain firm in what you believe
and to make some progress in faith.

Augustine

Sermon 59
THE OUR FATHER   Mt 6.9-13

In the course of their initiation, the catechumens have learned the 'I believe in God'. They have repeated it before all the Christians. Eight days later the Lord's prayer, the 'Our Father', is explained to them and they learn it.

Here Augustine is going to explain it to them. They must learn it and repeat it eight days later at the Vigil service on the night of Holy Saturday.

1 You have repeated what you must believe.
  Now hear
  what you must ask for in prayer.
  For you are not able to pray
  if you do not believe in God.
  Indeed, the Apostle said:
  'How can they pray to the Lord
  if they do not believe in him?'   Rom 10. 14
  Therefore you first learned the 'I believe in God',
  which is your rule of faith,, brief yet great.
  That rule is short because it has few words;
  it is great because the meaning of the words is weighty.
  The prayer that you hear and learn today
  you will repeat again in eight days.
  You have heard it already in the reading of the Gospel.
  It is the Lord himself who taught it to his apostles
  and it is through them that it has come to us.

Augustine

Indeed, one psalm says:
'Their voice has gone out into the whole world.' Ps 18 (19).4

— OUR FATHER IN HEAVEN

2   You have a Father in heaven.
So do not be attached to the earth.
Indeed, soon you are going to say:
'Our Father in heaven'.
You are going to belong to a large family.
Before this Father, rich and poor are brothers.
Before him, master and slave are brothers,
the general and the simple soldier are brothers.
On earth, Christians have fathers
who come from different positions in life.
Some fathers are well-known, others are not.
But all Christians pray to our Father who is in heaven.
If our Father is in heaven
there also our heritage is prepared for us. *
Our Father is generous.
So with him we shall possess
the riches that he gives so plentifully
He gives us our heritage
but he does not leave it to us by dying
in the way that earthly fathers do,
And he does not have to go away.
He remains always,
and waits for us to go to him.

And so we have learned of whom we should ask.
We learn now what we must ask,
so that we do not offend such a Father
by asking him wrongly.

---

* The Christian's heritage is promised at baptism. see Rev 21.6-7.

Augustine

3 What is it that the Lord Jesus Christ
   teaches us to ask our father in heaven ?
   — **MAY YOUR NAME BE HOLY**

What good is it to ask God
'May your name be holy' ?
The name of God is always holy.
So why do we ask him that his name should become holy ?
It is for us to be made holy by his Name.
Yes, the name of God is always holy
and we pray for it to be more holy in us.
When you are baptised
the name of God will be made holy in you.
After your baptism, why do you again pray for that ?
In order to guard the gift that you have received.

4 Another request comes next:
   — **MAY YOUR KINGDOM COME.**

If we ask for it
or if we do not ask for it,
the Kingdom of God will come.
Why do we ask for it, then ?
We ask for the Kingdom to come in us also,
as it will come in all God's friends.
We ask God to count us also among his friends
when he comes as King.

5 We say in the third request:
   — **MAY YOUR WILL BE DONE ON EARTH AS IT IS IN HEAVEN.**

What does that mean ?
We must serve God on earth
as the angels serve him in heaven.
The holy angels obey God,

they do not offend him,
they do lovingly what God asks.
So we desire also
to obey God lovingly.

You can also understand these words in another way:
Heaven in us is in our soul,
and the earth is our body.
So when we say:
'May your will be done on earth as in heaven',
we want to say:
Since we have heard the commandments of God,
our body is ready to obey.
Then, when body and spirit struggle against each other
we are still able to obey the commandments of God.
However, dear friends,
when the body struggles against the spirit. Gal 5.17
and the earth struggles against the sky,
the spirit must also struggle against the body.
Then the earth will not conquer the sky.
And if we are unable to avoid that struggle
we can refuse to yield to our bad desires.

There is again another way to understand that request:
'May your will be done on earth as in heaven'.
By their baptism,
Christians are like the man come from heaven,
that is to say, Christ.
We can then say that they are 'heavenly'.
On the other hand, those who do not believe in Christ
are like the earthly man * 1 Cor 15-17
and they are called 'earthly'.

---

* The earthly man is Adam. see Gen 2.7

Augustine

Then, when we say
'May your will be done on earth as in heaven',
we are saying to our very kind Father
"Bring the unbelievers to believe in you also
as we, the Christians, believe in you."
Thus we learn to pray for our enemies.

6 You then say in the prayer:
— GIVE US TODAY OUR DAILY BREAD.

By that we ask the Father
for what is necessary for our body,
meaning by 'bread' all that we need.

    The Bread of the Eucharist

However we can also understand our daily bread to be
the bread that you are going to receive in the Eucharist.
We do well to ask God to give it to us.
Indeed, what we ask then is
not to do evil, which can separate us from that Bread.

    The Bread of the Word

You listen to the Word of God each day.
That Word is also Bread.
It is not bread for the stomach
but it is food for the mind.
When this life is over we shall have no hunger:
we shall have no need of bread.
We shall have no need for the Eucharist.
Indeed, we shall be with Christ,
he who gives us his body to eat in the Eucharist.
We shall have no more need
to pronounce the words that we say to you,
nor to read the Bible.
We shall see in person the Word of the Father,
the Son of God.
Through him all has been made.

Augustine

> It is he who feeds the angels:
> he enlightens them, he teaches them wisdom.. *
> Indeed, the angels do not possess that wisdom
> by studying the words of a very difficult language:
> they drink in the unique Word.
> Filled with it they break out into song
> and they never stop singing God's praises.
> Indeed, one psalm says:
> 'Lord, they are happy
> who live in your house.
> They sing your praises without end.'   Ps 83(84).4

7 Therefore in this life we ask what follows:

— **FORGIVE US OUR OFFENCES.**

Baptism wipes out all the debts we have towards God,
that is, our sins.
However, no one is able to live here on earth
without sinning.   1 Jn 1.8
That wrong-doing is not always a great fault,
a fault that keeps us away from the bread. **
Yet, on this earth, no one is without fault.
And we are not able to receive baptism more than once.
So then, in the Lord's prayer
we have the means to wash away our faults daily.
One condition is:
it must make us do what we are going to say next.

— **AS WE FORGIVE THOSE WHO OFFEND US.**

And so I say to you,
you are going to become children of God.
You are not going to become children of a great man.

---

*   To enlighten is to give light and understanding to the mind.
**   Augustine is speaking of the Eucharist, Holy Communion.

Augustine

Is it some great personage
who is thinking of adopting you?
The love of God is making you all his children.
Each day you will say: "Our Father".
You will say that prayer even after baptism
and especially after baptism.
Yes, that prayer will only become truly prayer
after baptism.
In eight days you are going to repeat it
but you will not pray it yet.
After baptism, it will truly be your prayer.
Indeed, how can one who is not yet born *
be able to say: "Our Father"?
But after baptism you will say that prayer daily.
So then, I give you warning my brothers —
in the grace of God you are my children,
before the Father you are my brothers —
I say to you:
If someone offends you,
and that person comes and asks your pardon,
because he recognises his fault,
then you will forgive him everything with all your heart.
Otherwise you stop God from granting you forgiveness
when you go to ask pardon.
For if you yourselves do not forgive,
God will not forgive you.
That is why we ask for it now in this life
where sins are possible,
because in the other life there will be no sins we can forgive.
No one sins after death.
It will be too late then to say to God: Forgive as we forgive.
You must do your forgiving now in this life.

---

* This means the new birth of baptism. Jn 3.3-5

8 Next we pray saying:
— **DO NOT LEAD US INTO TEMPTATION**

It is essential for us not to give in to temptation —
indeed our life on earth is full of temptation —
and we must ask also to be delivered from evil
because there is much evil on earth.
When you say 'yes' to the tempter,
that is, to the evil spirit,
you are about to yield to temptation.
In fact, on this earth it is good to be tempted *
but it is not good to yield to temptation.
For example, someone wants to bribe you
so you are given money to do a bad action.
It is a temptation.
Yes, you long to have that money,
but it is also a proof of your uprightness
that you can give to God.
If you do not accept that money, you remain pure.
I will give you some advice:
scorn the desire to have money,
then money will not stain you.
Close the door to temptation and fasten the lock.
The lock is the love of God.

Without prayer
nobody is able to conquer temptation.
We need the help of God.
We are tempted in many ways.
We are tempted by gifts but also by threats.
When people cannot bribe us with money
they try to gain what they want through making us afraid.

---

* To be tempted is to be tested: when it is resisted by grace we grow stronger.

But if you are firmly attached to God,
God listens to your request:
'Do not lead us into temptation'.
Then, you obtain victory over your bad temptation
and over your fears.

So then, in the 'Our Father' there are seven requests in all.
Three requests are made for everlasting life with God,
and four for this present life.
'May your name be holy' —
that will be for ever.
'May your kingdom come' —
that kingdom will be for ever.
'May your will be done on earth as it is in heaven' —
that will be for ever.
'Give us today our daily bread' —
that will not be for ever.
'Forgive us our offences' —
that will not always be necessary.
'Do not lead us into temptation
but deliver us from evil' —
that will not always be necessary to ask,
but where there is temptation and where there is evil,
here on earth,
here we need to ask it.

Sermon Guelferbytanus 3
THE LORD'S PASSION

Each year on the day of the Lord's death, Good Friday, Christians assemble together. They read what is written in the Gospel about the Passion of the Lord Jesus.
Augustine explains it to his people.

1 The Passion of Jesus Christ, our Lord and Saviour,
is a guarantee to us of glory.
It teaches us about patience also. *
In our hearts we Christians are sure of God's grace,
Indeed it was for us that the only Son of God,
who lives always with the Father,
became a man like other men
and was born into a human family.
And for us, he even died by the hands of men
he himself had created.
The Lord has promised he will do great things for us.
What he did that we are remembering today was far greater.
What were we, when were we
when Christ died for sinners ?   Rom 5.6
He will give his life for those who belong to God
for he has already given us his death. Nobody can doubt it.

---

* The Passion of Our Lord is all the things he suffered at his death and bore with such patience. 'Passion' and 'patience' come from the same latin word meaning to suffer, to bear.

One day all human beings will be living with God:
we are weak, but can we hesitate to believe that?
Much more unbelievable
is what he has done already:
God died for human beings.
Who is Christ? He is the Word of the Father.
The Apostle John says:
'In the beginning the Word was with God.
The Word was with God and the Word was God.'   Jn 1.1
Nothing in him could die for us
so he took a human body
to die like us.

Although he could not die,
in that way he was able to die for us
and in that way he willed to give life to us
who must die.
He has made us sharers in what he is *
because he has first shared what we are.
We had nothing which could make us live,
he had nothing which could make him die.
So he made a wonderful exchange with us.
He has taken what belonged to us and has died.
He will give us what is his
and so we shall have life.
He is God and man.
He has made us. Our life is not our own but his.
To be like us he took our flesh which he had made
and so he died.

---

* He is God and we are made sharers in the life of God which is grace.

Augustine

2 Therefore we ought not to be ashamed
of the death of our Lord God.
We ought to have total confidence in it
and make it totally our glory.
He has indeed received from us
the death which he found in us
but he has faithfully promised to give us life.
That life is in him
and we are not able to have it through ourselves.
Yes, the Lord loves us so much.
He was sinless
yet he suffered for us sinners.
He has suffered what we have deserved by our sins.
So he will surely give to us
what he has given to God's friends.
He make the saints upright
and he will make us upright too.
The Apostle could see who hung there and for whom,
and to see so much humility in God
made his apostle expect heavenly glory for us....

3 We recognise and with great confidence we announce
that for us Christ was nailed to the cross.
Let us say it, not with fear, but with joy,
not with shame but with pride.
The apostle Paul saw in the Passion of Christ
a reason to glory,
and he recommends us to glory in it also.

Paul knew so many great things about Christ:
that he is God,
that he is with the Father
and it is he who created the world,

Augustine

and that he became a human being as we are,
yet he rules the world.
But Paul did not say that he gloried
in the marvellous things about Christ.
He said:
"I refuse to glory in anything
except in the cross of our Lord Jesus Christ."   Gal 6.14

4 And so let us glory in the cross of our Lord Jesus Christ.
Through the cross of Christ, the world is dead to us
and we are dead to the world.   Gal 6.14
We have traced the cross on our forehead
where shame usually shows,
so that we shall not be ashamed of it.... *

---

* When Christians make this sign on the forehead it shows that they are proud to belong to Christ. Learning to make the sign of the cross is the first thing a catechumen does.

Sermon 227
THE EUCHARIST

During the night of Holy Saturday, the newly baptised first receive the Eucharist, but St Augustine did not have time to speak to them at that moment. On Easter Day they gather and see the altar before them and on the altar the bread and wine to become the Body and Blood of Christ. Then Augustine speaks to them of the Eucharist (the Mass).

RECEIVE FREQUENTLY THE BODY AND BLOOD OF CHRIST

I have not forgotten my promise.
You came to receive Baptism
and I promised to speak to you
of the Body and Blood of Christ.
Last night you received the Eucharist
and now again you see on the altar the bread and the wine.
You must know what you have received.
You will receive it again and you should receive it daily.

You see this bread on the altar.
The Word of God has made it holy
and now it is the Body of Christ.
This cup, or rather the wine in the cup,
the Word of God has made holy
and now it is the Blood of Christ.
By this bread and this wine
the Lord Christ wills to hand over his Body and his Blood.
That blood he has poured out for us,

Augustine

and God forgives us our sins.
If you receive the Body and Blood of Christ
with a pure heart,
you are what you receive.

YOU ARE THE BODY OF CHRIST

Indeed, the Apostle Paul writes: 'We are many;
however there is only one bread
and so we form one body.' 1 Cor 10.17
That is how he explains the sacrament of the Lord's table:
there is only one bread, and although there are many of us,
we are only one Body.
This Bread shows how much you should love to be united.
Is bread made with one grain of wheat?
No, certainly. There were many grains of wheat,
but before they came together into bread, they were separate.
By water they were joined together
after they had been crushed.
If the wheat is not crushed into flour and mixed with water
it will not form what we call bread.
You also, in a certain way,
have been crushed like the grains of wheat
under the rock of fasting and of prayer
which drove out the spirit of evil.
Thus you became humble.
Then, you received baptism
and in a certain way the water of baptism
has made you become bread.
But does not bread need fire? What does the fire mean, then?
In a lamp, the oil feeds the fire.
For us, that oil is the sacrament of the Holy Spirit. *

---

* The sacrament of the Holy Spirit is Confirmation. The first Christians received at the same time Baptism, Confirmation and the Eucharist (Holy Communion).

Augustine

You will find he is able to help you to make progress.
When you gather together for the assembly in church,
stop useless talking : pay attention to the Holy Scriptures....
Reflect now, and observe
how the Holy Spirit came on the day of Pentecost.
This is how he came:
He showed himself in the shape of tongues
and these tongues were flames of fire.
The Holy Spirit makes us burn with love for God,
and transform the world. *
He burns up our straw - what is worthless in us -
and makes us pure as gold.
So the fire of the Holy Spirit comes after the water of Baptism
and you become the bread which is the Body of Christ,
and so in a way you become one.

HOW WE CELEBRATE THE EUCHARIST

After the prayer, we tell you to lift up- your hearts. **
That invitation is made to you as the members of Christ.
For indeed you have become the members of Christ,
but where is your Head ?
The body has members, but also a head.
If the head did not go first
the members would not be able to follow.
Where has Christ your head gone ?
What did you repeat in the 'I believe in God' ?
'The third day the Lord rose from the dead.
He ascended into heaven.
He is seated at the right hand of the Father.'
Therefore our head, the Lord, is in heaven.

---

* The world here means the forces which pull us away from God.
When gold was purified, it was first mixed with straw.
** This is the prayer after the readings from Scripture.

That is the reason, when we say:
"Lift up your hearts",
you reply:
"We lift them up to the Lord".
We are not able to turn our hearts toward the Lord,
neither by our own power, nor with what good we have done,
nor with our own efforts..
Indeed, God alone is able to give us
the power to turn our hearts to him.
For this reason, when the people have replied:
"We lift them up to the Lord"
the Bishop or the priest who is offering the sacrifice
continues by saying: "We give thanks to the Lord our God..."
We give thanks to Him
that we have our hearts turned toward the Lord
because without that gift of God
our hearts would be turned toward the earth.
And you agree with this by saying:
"It is right and good to give thanks to God".
He gives us the will
to raise our hearts toward the Lord, our Head.

Then, the bread and wine become
the Body and Blood of the Lord.
In that sacrifice offered to God,
God wants us to be ourselves his sacrifice.
That you can see clearly, since the bread and wine offered
represent us also.
After the bread and wine become the Body and Blood of Christ
we say the Lord's Prayer.
You have learned and repeated it.
Then you say: "Peace be with you."
Christians embrace each other as brothers and sisters.
That is the Sign of Peace.

Augustine

That sign of peace links you to one another,
So also your heart should not distance itself
from another's heart.

These then are the Sacraments, and very great ones.
We trust you with these mysteries on certain conditions.
Do you want to know what they are ?
The Apostle Paul said:
'Anyone who eats the bread of the Lord
or drinks from the cup unworthily
is responsible
for the Body and Blood of the Lord.'   1 Cor 11.27
What does it mean: to receive unworthily ?
It means to receive scornfully, to receive without respect.
Do not see the Bread and the Wine as something common
because of what you see with your eyes.
What you see is passing
but what it represents, and what you do not see,
does not pass away and is everlasting.
Indeed, you receive that Bread, you eat it, you swallow it.
But do you destroy the Body of Christ ?
Do you destroy the Church of Christ ?
Do you destroy the members of Christ ?
No, certainly not.

Here on earth, Christians become pure
because of the Body of Christ,
and in heaven they receive the glory of God.   Phil 3.20,21
So our union with Christ, represented here,
will remain for ever,
although the bread and wine you see
will disappear.

Receive therefore the Body of Christ
so that you will think like Christ,

so that you will keep unity in your heart,
and your heart will remain always fixed on the things above.
Do not put your hope in earthly things
but in those of heaven. Col 3.2
Let your faith in God be fire so that God will accept it.
Now you do not see, but you believe.
There in heaven on high you will see,
and then you will have joy without end.

Sermon 232
THE RESURRECTION

During Easter week, Augustine explained all the texts of the Gospel which speak of the living Jesus.
In this sermon he explains the passages in the Gospel according to Luke.

THE DISCIPLES ARE UNABLE TO BELIEVE

2 Now let us give our attention to what we have heard today.
Yesterday, I talked to you about the disciples' want of faith.
Today, Luke speaks again even more clearly.
Thus we will understand
how great God's gift to us is:
though we have not seen, yet we believe. Jn 20.29

Jesus has called his disciples.
He has instructed them, he has loved them on earth.
He did so many extraordinary things for them to see.
Then he raised people from the dead.
Yet the disciples were unable to believe
that Jesus could raise his own body from the dead.

THE DISCIPLES DO NOT BELIEVE THE WOMEN

The women came to the tomb.
They did not find the body in the tomb.
They heard angels say:
"The Lord has risen from the dead."
Then the women went to announce this to the men.

And then what does the text say ? What did you hear ?
'These words seemed foolish to them.'   Lk 24.11
How weak we humans are.
When Eve told what the serpent said to her   Gen 3.6
she was heard at once.
The words of a false woman are believed
but she led us to death.
Here are some women who speak what is true
so that we may have life
and no one believes them.
If we cannot believe a woman
why did Adam believe Eve ?
If we can believe a woman
why did not the disciples believe the holy women ?
Notice here the goodness of the Lord.
Our Lord Jesus has willed
that women first announce his resurrection.
Why is that ?
It was a woman who made us fall into sin.
It is also a woman who has restored us to uprightness.
Yes, it was a young woman who gave Christ to the world.
These also are women
who announce his resurrection from the dead.
A woman gave death,
a woman gave life.
But the disciples did not believe
what the women were saying to them.
They thought it was madness.
Yet what they were announcing was true.

THE DISCIPLES AT EMMAUS

3 Now see: Lk 4.13-35
two disciples are walking along the road.
They were speaking about the events in Jerusalem,

about the death of Christ.
They were walking along and talking
and they were sad because he was dead
and they did not know that he had risen from the dead.
Jesus himself appeared,
a third traveller walked with them
and joined in their conversation.
But their eyes were not open,
they were kept from recognising him.
For it was necessary for their hearts to be better instructed
by his words.
So they recognised him only later.
For the moment,
Jesus asks them what they are talking about together.
He wants to make them say what he already knows.
You have heard
how the disciples were astonished at his question,
because it was such a well-known matter.
Yet Jesus seemed not to know about it.
They said to him:
" All the travellers to Jerusalem
know what has happened at this time
and do you alone not know ? "
He asked them : " What, then ?"
The disciples answered him:
"What happened to Jesus of Nazareth:
he was a prophet
powerful by his works and his deeds." Lk 24.19
What are you saying, disciples ?
(Here Augustine is speaking directly to the disciples at Emmaus.)
You say that Christ is a prophet.
You are Jews and should know better than that.
No, he is the Master of the prophets.

Augustine

WHO IS THE SON OF MAN?

They had taken the words of others.
What do I mean, the words of others?
You remember, when Jesus asked his disciples:
"What do people say
that I, the Son of Man, am?" * Mt 16.13-19
They told him what other people thought:
"Some say that you are Elijah.
Others say you are John the Baptist.
Others again say Jeremiah or one of the other prophets."
These were the words of other people,
not the disciples' words.
Then Jesus said to them:
"And you, what do you say? Who am I?
You have told me the opinion of other people.
I want to hear what you believe yourselves."
Then Peter spoke for them all, because they were united.
"You are Christ, the Son of the living God."
Not just one of the prophets, but the Son of the living God.
"You do what the prophets have foretold.
It is you who have created the angels.
You are the Christ, the Son of the living God."

Then Peter has the honour to learn
from the mouth of Jesus himself:
"Simon, son of John, you are blessed.
Indeed it is not through human knowledge
that you have known this.
It is through my Father who is in heaven.
And I say to you: 'You are Peter,

---

* Son of Man: In the Old Testament we already find this expression meaning the Messiah that God would send.

and on this rock I will build my Church.
And the power of the underworld will not overcome it.
I will give you the keys of the kingdom of heaven,
and what you loose on earth,
will be loosed in heaven.'" Mt 16.13-19
Peter deserved that praise because of his faith.
He did not speak like any other men then.
He spoke the truth...

JESUS SAID TO PETER: YOU ARE BLESSED BY GOD. HE ALSO CALLED HIM SATAN. WHY ?

4   Directly after these words,
Jesus announced his Passion and death to the disciples.
Peter was afraid and said:
"No, Lord. That must never be !"
Then Jesus turned and said to Peter:
 "Get behind me, Satan." Mt 16.21-23
Jesus called Peter 'Satan'.
Where now are the words spoken a moment earlier ?
Is Satan blessed ?
Peter is blessed when he listens to God.
He is Satan when he thinks in an earthly way.
Afterwards the Lord explains
why he called him Satan.
"You do not know the things of God.
You only understand what is earthly."
Why was he blessed before ?
Because what he said, God had revealed to him.
Why was he Satan afterwards ?
'You do not know the things of God.'
When you did appreciate them you were blessed.
But what you understand is earthly.

See how the disciples changed their minds
almost from one time and place to the next
One minute they stood firm,
the next they fell.
One minute their minds were in the light,
the next in darkness,
because the things of God brought understanding,
but their own thinking brought darkness.
How did the light come ?
'Look to the Lord
and you will shine in his light.' Ps 33 (34).5

8 Very dear friends,
yesterday I said to you and I will say it again today:
Christ risen from the dead is in us
if we live well.
Our old bad life must die.
We must go forward each day in our new life ....